Ecologies of Internet Video

This book explores the complex, dynamic, and contested webs of relationships in which three different groups of video makers found themselves when distributing their work on the Internet. It draws upon both the Deleuzian notion of "assemblage" and Actor-Network Theory, which together provide a rich conceptual framework for characterizing and analysing these webs. The groups examined are a UK video activist project, a community of film and television fans originating in the US, and an association of US community television producers.

Rather than taking YouTube as its point of departure, this book centres on the groups themselves, contextualizing their contemporary distribution practices within their pre-Internet histories. It then follows the groups as they drew upon various Internet technologies beyond YouTube to create their often-complex video distribution assemblages, a process that entangled them in these webs of relationships.

Through the analysis of detailed ethnographic fieldwork conducted across a period of several years, this book demonstrates that while the groups found some success in achieving their various goals as video makers, their situations were often problematic and their agency limited, with their practices contested by both human and technological actors within their distribution assemblages.

John Hondros is a Visiting Lecturer at the School of Media, Film and Music at the University of Sussex, UK. Prior to his academic career, he held various senior roles in the digital media industry, pioneering the development of multiplatform television and Internet video internationally.

Routledge Research in Cultural and Media Studies

For a full list of titles in this series, please visit www.routledge.com.

Ecologies of Internet Video
Beyond YouTube

John Hondros

LONDON AND NEW YORK

First published 2018
by Routledge

2 Park Square, Milton Park, Abingdon, Oxfordshire OX14 4RN
52 Vanderbilt Avenue, New York, NY 10017

*Routledge is an imprint of the Taylor & Francis Group, an
informa business*

First issued in paperback 2020

Library of Congress Cataloging-in-Publication Data
CIP data has been applied for.

ISBN: 978-1-138-89556-0 (hbk)
ISBN: 978-0-367-59021-5 (pbk)

Typeset in Sabon
by codeMantra

Contents

Preface

The origin of this book, and the beginning of my interest in the relationship between the Internet and video, can be traced to 1997 when I first saw WebTV in operation. This was a television set top box that contained a dial-up modem to access the Internet, which it would display on a television screen, and an analogue tuner for receiving broadcast television programmes. What particularly fascinated me about this device was how it integrated in various ways Internet interactivity with the television programmes being broadcast. I had just begun working in the then nascent digital media industry, and my early experience with this technology inspired me to focus my career in this new, integrated domain. Over the next 14 years, I worked on various projects in this area, and in that time, the industry's focus shifted away from WebTV-type technologies to ones like YouTube that concerned distributing video via the Internet. My fascination with this marriage of the Internet and video remained, however, and in fact intensified as Internet video distribution technologies became more widespread, although my interest shifted from the commercial and technological concerns that preoccupied the industry to sociological ones. In particular, I wanted to understand the social dynamics within which this new technology was becoming entangled. While this book takes a sociological approach to the problem, it is also informed by the various perspectives, insights, and sensibilities gained during my industry experience, and therefore draws upon 20 years of reflection upon the relationship between video and the Internet.

Over 100 people, belonging to the groups of video makers discussed in the following pages, directly contributed to the primary research that forms the basis of this book. Many of the insights contained within it depended upon their generosity, both in granting me access to the inner workings of their groups and in giving up their time to help me understand their practices. This book is therefore dedicated to them, and to their determination in pursuing their goals as video makers in the face of often considerable resistance and difficulties.

1   Introduction

This book explores the complex, dynamic, and contested webs of relationships that three different groups of non-professional video makers
found themselves in when distributing their work on the Internet.[1] These
webs can be thought of metaphorically as ecologies, and they will be
framed and analysed in the following chapters using the concepts of
assemblages and actor-networks. Through this analysis we will see that
while these groups found varying degrees of success in achieving their
goals as video makers, their situations were often problematic and precarious, and their agency limited, with their practices contested by other
actors often considerably more powerful than themselves as they went
about their task of distributing their videos online.

While YouTube was the primary focus for social scientists investigating Internet video when the initial plan for this book was formulated
in 2009, and continues to remain so to this day, a different approach
is used here. Rather than taking YouTube or even the Internet in general as a point of departure, this book instead centres on categories of
producers who existed prior to the advent of the Internet, but who later
adopted it as a distribution technology. The reason for this approach is
that it frames Internet video distribution technologies within the wider
historical context of video distribution technologies in general, rather
than treating them as something unprecedented. Given the ethnographic
method used here (discussed below), this also left open the possibility of
encountering producers who had some experience with pre-Internet distribution methods, opening lines of enquiry concerning the relationship
between online and offline video distribution methods. This approach,
while focusing on Internet technologies, therefore also invites comparisons with pre-Internet methods, providing a different perspective on this
technology from ones that begin with YouTube or the Internet as their
point of departure.

The three groups of video producers that are the subject of this book
are the California Community Media Exchange, an association of US
community media centres located in Northern California; visionOntv,
the London-based Internet video project of the UK activist group Undercurrents; and a group of film and television fans who were active on

the LiveJournal journaling website. These groups were selected through the application of a number of criteria: First, they belonged to categories of producers that were prominent in the academic literature on the pre-Internet era, for the reasons just discussed above, and qualifying categories were further restricted to those that concerned the activities of non-professional producers, since this book's focus is on the participatory aspects of the technology. Second, the ethnographic approach followed here required that the groups were all actively producing and distributing videos during the period of the research, to allow for observations of, and participation in, their activities. To leave open the possibility of being able to observe and participate with these groups at offline as well as online locations, they also needed to be accessible, both in terms of travel time and cost, from my base in London, and to some degree to each other. Third, to allow for the in-depth interaction with the producers and their various online and offline traces and artefacts that is required for ethnographic work without having to trouble translators, the groups also needed to operate primarily in English.

The ethnographic method was chosen for this research as it is both well suited to the subject matter and also promised to provide a rich, contextualized, and robust empirical data set for later analysis. Writing in 2000, Miller and Slater felt the need to defend their use of ethnography in the opening lines of their self-consciously entitled book *The Internet: An Ethnographic Approach*: "Why should we do an ethnography of the Internet ...? Because – contrary to the first generation of Internet literature – the Internet is not a monolithic or placeless 'cyberspace'; rather, it is numerous new technologies, used by diverse people, in diverse real-world locations. Hence, there is everything to be gained by an ethnographic approach, by investigating how Internet technologies are being understood and assimilated somewhere in particular" (2000, 1). Since then, ethnographic approaches to Internet use have become commonplace amongst researchers (although the dualistic notion of the Internet as a virtual space separated from the material world still persists in various forms today).

Ethnography's advocates cite amongst its strengths "the richness of its data and insights, its ability to integrate the study of text and viewer", and how it situates these within their relevant contexts (Press and Livingstone 2006, 176). Hine emphasizes the contextual benefits of an ethnographic approach when she observes that it "allows researchers to study social situations on their own terms. The key idea is that the researcher should become immersed in the social situation being studied and should use that experience to try to learn how life is lived there, rather than coming in with a particular pre-formed research question or assumptions about the issues that will be of interest. Ethnography is thought of as the most open of research approaches, which adapts itself to the social situations that it finds" (2009, 6). The benefits of this immersive approach for studies of the Internet lay in its ability to "engage deeply with technologies and with the people designing and using them ... The results are studies that illuminate the social dynamics at the heart of the technologies concerned" (Hine 2009, 12). It has also been argued that "ethnographic methods are actually quite well suited to study Internet sociality, given the recent theoretical debates in anthropology about multiple identities and dynamism of communities" (Beaulieu 2004, 143). Given that online video as a phenomenon was only a few years old at the time this project was conceived and undergoing rapid change, with few empirical studies of it in existence, a methodological approach that respected our ignorance of this medium by approaching the people that used it openly and adaptably through immersion in their activities as video producers, and which promised detailed insights into their little-understood social dynamics, therefore seemed well suited to this project.

Hammersley and Atkinson summarize the basic elements of ethnographic data collection: "Ethnography usually involves the researcher participating, overtly or covertly, in people's daily lives for an extended period of time, watching what happens, listening to what is said, and/ or asking questions through informal and formal interviews, collecting documents and artefacts" (2007, 3). Defining the boundaries of the ethnographic field, that is the space where this data collection takes place, raises questions concerning the relationship between online and offline spaces. This book takes the position, advocated by a number of other scholars,[2] that there is no sharp separation between them and that "online and offline practices and spaces are co-constituted, hybridized, and embedded within one another" (Leander and Mckim 2003, 223) and follows Hine's advice that the ethnographer should engage "in relevant practices wherever they might be found" (2009, 12) and "find ways of immersing themselves in life as it is lived online, and as it connects through into offline social spheres" (2005, 18).

The data collection for this book took place over two separate periods of fieldwork, from May 2011 to June 2012, and then again from November 2016 to November 2017, providing snapshots of the groups' video distribution practices during these two periods and allowing for an investigation into how these practices evolved over time. For the first period of the fieldwork, and for the first three months of the second period, I observed and participated with my informants either online or offline on nearly a daily basis and did this on a weekly basis for the remainder of the second period. The use of a mix of data collection techniques during the fieldwork enabled not only the compilation of a rich data set, but also a robust one whose validity was tested by the triangulation of the data collected, comparing the results obtained from one collection technique against those of another.

These techniques included 85 formal interviews with 61 informants conducted face-to-face, by telephone/Skype, and by email. I also participated

with and observed my informants at 26 different offline events and locations including conferences, demonstrations, training workshops, exhi-
bitions, conventions, and community media centres. My participation at
these events and locations included assisting my informants with different
aspects of their video production work, speaking on a panel at a fan convention, producing my own community video at one of the community
media centres for broadcast on their public access television channel, and
generally becoming involved in the activities of my informants in these
places. I also engaged in informal discussions with these 61 informants
throughout my time at these venues, as well as engaging in informal conversations with over 50 others who were also present.

Observations of my informants' online activities included viewing the
videos and images they uploaded to different sites; reading their posts on
social networking sites, blogs, and bulletin boards; reading the comments
left on their videos on the different hosting and social networking sites
where they appeared; and examining the other traces associated with
their online activity such as "likes" and video view counts. My participation in their online activities included leaving text comments and "likes"
on their videos and posts, making my own posts, and replying to their
comments on my comments and posts. I added them, and was added by
them, to friends lists on the different platforms they used, engaged in
real-time text chat with some of them on these platforms, and helped test
versions of the software platforms they were developing themselves.

A policy of full disclosure was adopted towards all the informants for
both the offline and online participant observer activities undertaken,
whereby my identity and the nature of the research were disclosed to
them all directly. In the situations where the informants engaged in
online spaces with others that I did not have direct contact with, an
introduction to the research was posted in the relevant space where appropriate, and the observations concerning these others are only referred
to in general terms and in an aggregated form throughout this book.

The large, diverse, and detailed data set collected using these techniques allowed for not only the triangulation of, for example, an informant's interview responses against their online activity and traces,
and of one informant's interview response concerning a question about
their group with the response of another, but it also allowed for a triangulation of informants' responses over time, with some being formally
interviewed up to three times over the course of the research (at both the
beginning and end of the first fieldwork period, and then again during
the second period). My immersion in the groups over this extended period also resulted in the building of considerable trust with many of
them, which allowed for some frank discussions to take place near the
end of the first fieldwork period in particular, in addition to creating
an environment that allowed for many informal offline and online exchanges to take place, which provided additional triangulation points

for the data set collected. All these sources taken together enabled me to critically assess what I was told, saw, and otherwise experienced, and the ethnographies presented in the following chapters should therefore be understood as critical accounts and syntheses of the collected data.

The general structure of this book is as follows: Chapter 2 introduces each of the three producer groups that are the book's primary subjects and contextualizes them within the literature on their respective video genres: activist video, film and television fan videos, and public access television. The literature discussed in this chapter covers the state of these genres both before and after the advent of the Internet so as to situate each group in its broader historical context, for the reasons already noted above. The final section of this chapter examines some general aspects of online video distribution to supplement the context provided by the chapter's genre-based discussion.

Chapter 3 introduces the theoretical framework used in subsequent chapters to analyse the ethnographies of the three producer groups. This framework draws upon both Actor-Network Theory (ANT) and Manuel DeLanda's reading of Gilles Deleuze and Felix Guattari's notion of assemblages, conceptualizing social wholes as formed of heterogeneous elements. In the context of this book, these social wholes are the complex arrangements of humans, computers, and other components involved in the production, distribution, and reception of the subject groups' videos. This theoretical framework also concerns itself with the relationships that exist between these components and the various processes that stabilize and destabilize these relationships. The chapter begins by outlining the circumstances behind the adoption of this framework, showing how it was prompted by the limited ability of humanistic approaches to online video, which dominated academic discourse in the years leading up to this book, to account for some initial encounters in the field. In addition to providing a detailed discussion of both ANT and DeLanda's Assemblage Theory, the chapter also examines how these two theories have been used to understand digital media phenomena by other scholars, reviews some criticisms of the theories, and finally examines the ways that they complement each other, showing how adopting a combined approach allows for a more nuanced analysis of the ethnographies that follow.

Chapters 4, 5, and 6 each provide an ethnographic account of one of the three producer groups, analysing each account within the theoretical framework presented in Chapter 3. These chapters examine the typically complex arrangements of humans, machines, and other elements that different producers created to distribute their videos, highlighting the often precarious and problematic nature of these. They provide detailed accounts of why these producers made videos, why they chose the particular technologies they did to distribute them, and how they used these to interact with their audiences and otherwise achieve their goals, focusing on the causes of their successes, failures, and frustrations in pursuit of these goals.[3] These chapters go into considerable detail concerning the producers' activities because, as will be discussed in Chapter 3, the kinds of explanations that are possible using the theoretical framework of this book are inductive, emerging "bottom-up" from the specifics of the sociological situations under investigation, rather than being deduced from a theoretical position decided upon in advance and applied "top-down" onto the situations in question. A crucial emergent theme from these chapters concerns the question of agency, and the various threads of discussion concerning this from them are drawn together in Chapter 7, which examines how the groups' and individual producers' agency was entangled within the dynamics of the complex and contested webs of heterogeneous relationships of which they were a part as they pursued their goals.

Notes

1 The term "video maker" is used interchangeably with the terms "video producer" or simply "producer" throughout the following chapters. For simplicity's sake, "video" is used in a general sense in this book to refer to any relevant moving image capture or display medium, such as celluloid film, videotape, solid state storage, and LCD displays.

2 See for example the surveys of the ethnographic studies of the Internet conducted by Orgad (2009), Leander and Mckim (2003), and Garcia et al. (2009).

3 The term "audience" is used throughout to refer to people who watch videos or who use the different technologies discussed below to access and interact with those videos or who use them to engage with their producers or other audience members. An audience member or producer will sometimes be referred to as a "user" in contexts where this makes for clearer prose, such as when their interactions with a particular kind of technology is under discussion. Hybrid terms like "prod-user" have been avoided, as the conventional terms of "producer", "audience", and "user" are sufficient for what follows, and any hybridity in behaviour will be addressed in context where relevant.

References

Beaulieu, A. 2004. "Mediating Ethnography: Objectivity and the Making of Ethnographies of the Internet." *Social Epistemology* no. 18 (2):139–163.

Garcia, A.C., A.I. Standlee, J. Bechkoff, and Y. Cui. 2009. "Ethnographic Approaches to the Internet and Computer-Mediated Communication." *Journal of Contemporary Ethnography* no. 38 (1):52–84.

Hammersley, M., and P. Atkinson. 2007. *Ethnography: Principles in Practice.* Abingdon: Taylor & Francis.

Hine, Christine. 2005. "Research Relationships and Online Relationships: Introduction." In *Virtual Methods: Issues in Social Research on the Internet,* edited by Christine Hine, 17–20. Oxford: Berg.

Hine, Christine. 2009. "How Can Qualitative Internet Researchers Define the Boundaries of Their Projects?" In *Internet Inquiry: Conversations about Method*, edited by A.N. Markham and N.K. Baym, 1–20. Thousand Oaks, CA: Sage.

Leander, Kevin M., and Kelly K. Mckim. 2003. "Tracing the Everyday 'Sitings' of Adolescents on the Internet: A Strategic Adaptation of Ethnography across Online and Offline Spaces." *Education, Communication & Information* no. 3 (2):211–240.

Miller, D., and D. Slater. 2000. *The Internet: An Ethnographic Approach*. Oxford: Berg.

Orgad, S. 2009. "The Interrelations between 'Online' and 'Offline': Questions, Issues and Implications." In *The Oxford Handbook of Information and Communication Technologies*, edited by R. Mansell, C. Avgerou, D. Quah, and R. Silverstone, 514–536. Oxford: Oxford University Press.

Press, Andrea, and Sonia Livingstone. 2006. "Taking Audience Research into the Age of New Media: Old Problems and New Challenges." In *Questions of Method in Cultural Studies*, edited by S. Livingstone, A. Press, M. White, and J. Schwoch, 175–200. Malden, MA: Blackwell.

2 Activist, Fan, and Community Video before and after the Internet

As we saw in the introductory chapter, rather than taking the Internet as its point of departure, this book instead centres on three groups of producers who were drawn from video genres that existed in the pre-Internet era and who were also actively engaged in distributing their videos on the Internet when the fieldwork for this study was being carried out.[1] This chapter reviews the state of these genres both before and after the advent of the Internet to provide a historical and contemporary context for the groups' video distribution practices that will be examined in the ethnography chapters that follow.[2]

The first three sections of this chapter each concern one of the three genres – activist video, film and television fan videos, and public access television – beginning with a brief introduction of the relevant producer group, followed by a sketch of the pre-Internet era technologies and practices related to their genre, and finishing with a discussion of the state of the genre in the Internet-era. Since the literature for some of these genres is broad ranging, the discussion in these sections will be limited to material that is most relevant to providing context for the group in question by restricting the discussion to particular subgenres, geographic regions, or illustrative examples, as required. The reason for the use of genres here is not an attempt to demark sharp boundaries around the different video making groups, but simply to provide a general framework to help organize the literature around them to ensure that they are contextualized in the appropriate way.

The fourth section departs from the genre-based approach of the first three sections and looks at some general aspects of online video distribution to provide additional context for the ethnography chapters, focusing on community formation and practices and the power relations that exist between users and the different platforms they use.

Activist Video

VisionOntv began development in 2008 as a project of the video activist group Undercurrents with the purpose of promoting social change through the Internet using video. In 2009 it was incorporated as a separate limited company, jointly owned by Undercurrents; the Joseph Rowntree Reform Trust, which was the venture's funder; and the two visionOntv founders Hamish, who was also a member of Undercurrents, and Richard, a former BBC television investigative journalist.[3] Vision-Ontv engaged in a number of activities to achieve their purpose: it made activist videos for distribution on the Internet, it distributed its own and other people's activist videos on the Internet, it developed and maintained its own online video distribution platform, and it trained other people in how to make activist videos and distribute them on the Internet. It also developed its platform as a model for other video activists to adopt.

This section develops a context for visionOntv by reviewing elements of the literature on activist video. While there is considerable debate concerning the definition or even the correct name for this genre (Atkinson 2010, 13; Atton 2002, 9; Bailey et al. 2008, 30; Dowmunt 2007, 3; Kenix 2011, 7; Waltz 2005, 2), the focus here will be on a category of video producers who are defined as being in opposition to or challenging the hegemony of mainstream media (Couldry and Curran 2003, 7; Sandoval and Fuchs 2010) and who, like visionOntv, have "social change at their heart" (Atton 2002, 19) and "challenge power structures and attempt to transform social roles" (Atkinson 2010, 22).[4]

Activist video before the Internet. While the genre of activist video in the UK can trace its roots to earlier decades,[5] the groups that emerged in the late 1960s signalled its "sudden flowering", with the countercultural movements of that time providing fertile ground for their growth (Dickinson 1999, 17). Fountain surveys the groups that pioneered the genre during this period:

> The London Film Makers' Co-op ... began in 1966 and became the focal point for ... political experimentation for the next decade and beyond ... The Amber Film Collective was founded in Newcastle in 1968 and dedicated its work to an exploration and expression of working-class life and culture in that region ... Cinema Action, a left collective which worked closely with radical elements of the trades union movement ... the Berwick Street Collective, a left group concerned with allying formal difference with militant content ... and Liberation Films ..., a production and distribution group closely associated with the anti-Vietnam War movement and the women's liberation movement.
>
> (2007, 31)

These groups, later to become known as "workshops", typically "began with a few like-minded people getting together round shared objectives", with their activities integrating the "production, distribution and exhibition of films", although they differed somewhat in organization and approach. For example, while the London Film Makers' Co-op was "a cultural centre and facility serving an open membership ... of individual film-makers, ... the collectives, like Cinema Action or Amber, consisted of fewer members who worked together as a team and also provided facilities and equipment to other people but on an *ad hoc* basis, and at the discretion of the team" (Dickinson 1999, 41). While these were originally volunteer organizations, "funding agencies on the regional and national levels combined their money with the new Channel 4 to resource production" (Thomas 2012, 196), which led to a rapid growth in their number, from around 30 such workshops by the late 1970s to over 100 by the late 1980s (Dickinson 1999, 68–69). This rapid rise was attended by an even more rapid decline precipitated by changes in the funding model between 1988 and 1991 that few workshops survived (Thomas 2012, 196).

The integrated practice of the workshops with respect to the production, distribution, and exhibition of films is illustrated by Amber, who organized "their activities around documenting the excluded regional and class experience ... [with] the active participation of the local community" and where the screening of the finished films within the community were an essential part of the film-making process. Their approach thus rejected "the Fordist segmentation of industrial film-making" (Thomas 2012, 197). Amber in fact devoted considerable time and resource to distributing their films: They maintained a small cinema in Newcastle, and they also screened their films at local group meetings, such as those of the Labour Party, and at workplaces, where the screenings were organized through the trade unions. Amber considered discussion and debate post-screening an important part of the process and would sometimes favour shorter films over longer ones as they found these led to more discussion. They also had plans to show their films via a closed video circuit within the public spaces of areas run by local government authorities, such as in the waiting rooms of social security offices, but this did not come to fruition as the UK central government at the time prevented local authorities from engaging in political activity (Dickinson 1999, 253–254).

For the workshops in general, Channel 4 television, as well as being a funding partner, was also a distribution medium for their films, broadcasting them for much of the 1980s (Thomas 2012, 196). The workshops also began to adopt videotapes as a distribution method in the 1980s, moving away from the more personal screening practices for reasons to do with cost and the changing face of alternative politics in the UK (Dickinson 1999, 67).

Undercurrents, the parent organization of visionOntv, emerged as a video activist group just after the end of the workshop movement. It began in 1993 as Small World Media, founded by "two disillusioned television producers and a group of activists ... to explore the potential of using domestic Hi8 camcorders to bring about social and environmental change" (Undercurrents 2017a). It eventually took on the name of its primary output, a video magazine called *Undercurrents*, which was a self-described "alternative news video" released on videocassette tape. The first issue, for example, contained six videos that ran for an hour and a quarter in total and included a segment called "Street News", which was "a roundup of stories that television ignores, marginalises or fails to cover"; "a four part film highlighting how the Criminal Justice Bill affects the activities of protestors, ravers, travellers and squatters"; and a documentary on anti-roads campaigners (Undercurrents 2017b).

Undercurrents's audience contributed content for these video magazines, and calls to action were on the back cover of the tapes. These were "both a call to video action for the campaigning community and an offer of space to publicise their cause, the potential of gaining a place on Undercurrents' news agenda and rolling out to fellow campaigners and activists" (Heritage 2008, 139). Undercurrents used various strategies to distribute the video magazines: The videocassettes were available by post via mail order and subscription and also directly from Undercurrents's members at various events (Harding 1998, 85; Heritage 2008, 155). Undercurrents also encouraged their audience, through interstitial calls to action within the videos themselves, to share their videos with others and to host screenings in their community (Heritage 2008, 155). In addition, the tapes were delivered to established news organizations in an attempt to gain a mainstream audience, and two compilation videos were in fact shown by Channel Four television (Heritage 2008, 99; Waltz 2005, 52). Beyond relying on videotape, Undercurrents also set up screenings throughout the UK when each new edition of the video magazine was released (Waltz 2005, 53).

In addition to the production and distribution of the video magazines, Undercurrents also set up an archive of the videos they produced and of those that were sent to them by other video activists and campaigners and also provided training in shooting and editing to would-be activist video makers (Harding 1998, 98; Heritage 2008, 150).

Activist video in the Internet era. There is a large and growing literature on online activist video and so the discussion here, like the one above, will be restricted to a few examples and themes most relevant to visionOntv's circumstances and practices. The first of these examples is a continuation of the discussion of Undercurrents from above. Following the release of their last video magazine in 1999, Undercurrents began to experiment with online video. Their first attempt involved online video streaming of events from the Carnival Against Capitalism in London in 1999. The audience numbers were very low however, and Undercurrents came to the conclusion that online video's time had not yet come, and it would not be until some years later that they engaged with it again in earnest (O'Connor, 2011).

While visionOntv had begun as Undercurrents's online video project in 2008, with it being spun-off as a separate entity in 2009 (operated by different personnel and located in London rather than Swansea), Undercurrents continued to develop their own online video presence separately from it. By late 2011, Undercurrents had experimented with several different online video platforms, but they had finally settled on Blip and YouTube, and would feed videos from these into their Facebook page via an RSS feed. Undercurrents, however, had an ambivalent attitude toward these platforms. For example, with regard to Facebook, there were concerns about how it separated itself off from the rest of the Internet and about its desire to control user data, since these were contrary to Undercurrents's principles. Similarly, while acknowledging that they felt compelled to be on YouTube because of its very large share of the online video audience, there were concerns about it being a corporate-owned entity, and therefore part of an ethos that Undercurrents actively opposed, and about the risk it may censor videos that were critical of this ethos (O'Connor, 2011).

YouTube was also an important part of many other activist video producers' online distribution activities. Presence (2015, 193) argues these kinds of organizations, like Undercurrents, struggle with "the contradictions involved in using capitalist media organisations to host anticapitalist content". Some scholars have in fact questioned the suitability of such spaces for activist media, citing corporate exploitation of social networking labour, state surveillance, and corporate and state censorship as sources of concern (see for example, Costanza-Chock 2008). These political concerns, along with the more mundane one of finding ways to stand out from the massive array of content on these platforms, mean that some alternative video makers "tend to use YouTube and similar platforms as a means of advertising their own site, or as an easy means of hosting videos which can then be embedded elsewhere" (Presence 2015, 193).

Some have found YouTube problematic for other reasons. For example, Fenton and Barassi's (2011) study of the Cuba Solidarity Campaign (CSC) discusses the frustration campaigners felt concerning "the individualistic logic of social media". This frustration arose from the belief that "individual messages are often given the same importance as the messages that have arisen out of the tensions and negotiations of a collective of people", resulting in the messages produced by such collectives getting lost in the "information overload of the online space". The CSC had therefore rejected the use of interactivity in their social media practices, including their use of YouTube: "When the CSC opened its YouTube account, [they] chose not to allow others to post comments beneath their videos", although this choice "was not motivated by a will to be undemocratic, but by the fact that they 'simply couldn't afford interactivity' ... because ... the CSC did not have the resources to reply to individual messages that appeared beneath their videos. This was considered to be a real problem for the campaign because often individual messages would constitute a challenge to the one of the organization but the lack of time and resources prevented organizers from engaging with such discussions" (Fenton and Barassi 2011, 187).

Others have also pointed to the limitations of YouTube as a platform for alternative social and political discussion, consensus building, and mobilization. Juhasz (2008, 305–306) argues, for example, that both the space limitations and the culture associated with commenting on YouTube are not conducive to the kinds of discursive practices required for such activities, and that the platform's search algorithm's apolitical contextualization of videos undermines their critical voice and therefore also their ability to raise political and social consciousness. Hess's findings on the responses made to videos on YouTube, either in the form of text comment or as videos made to respond to the original video, support and elaborate upon Juhasz's position. Hess (2009) analysed the responses to videos posted on YouTube by the Office of National Drug Control Policy (ONDCP) in the US promoting prohibition of recreational drug use. He argues that while there were in fact some comments and video responses produced as resistance to the ONDCP's message and to encourage democratic deliberation, they were lost "in a mix of jokes, pseudonyms, and user flaming". Hess argues therefore that "YouTube does not offer a concrete and fully deliberative environment largely due to its overwhelming structure and use for entertainment ... digital activism is limited in the sea of responses, replies, and [the] often dismissive and overly playful atmosphere ... scholarship regarding digital activism should rethink the nature of this medium ... in regard to [its] ability to affect change" (2009, 412).

Some, on the other hand, see YouTube as playing an important part in alternative social and political movements. For example, Uldam and Askanius (2013, 1200), while acknowledging that the practices of YouTube commenting do indeed impede constructive social and political discussion, found in their study of a video calling for protest at a UN climate change conference in Denmark that "by providing a space for discussions on the politics of climate change, the debates on YouTube did extend the discursive opportunities opened up by the ... conference ..., facilitating debate between otherwise disparate publics", such as between activists and "ordinary citizens" and "between radical and reformist factions of the environmental movement". Many have also seen YouTube as playing an important role in mobilizing support for the so-called "Arab Spring" uprisings. For example, Howard et al. (2011, 2), while acknowledging that the Arab Spring had many causes, argue "one of these sources was social media and its power to put a human face on political oppression. Bouazizi's self immolation was one of several stories told and retold on Facebook, Twitter, and YouTube in ways that inspired dissidents to organize protests, criticize their governments, and spread ideas about democracy". For them, YouTube was "a particularly important tool for spreading news and information of Egypt's uprising – in the form of user-generated videos – around the world", and while they did not measure the actual impact of these videos, they believe "some images of suffering certainly would have spurred protests and heightened moral outrage" (Howard et al. 2011, 22).

Looking beyond YouTube and other corporate video aggregators, some activist video makers have turned to different kinds of online distribution platforms. One such example is the KEIN.org portal, which emerged from the "Kein Mensch ist illegal" (Nobody Is Illegal) campaign beginning in 1997 in Kassel in Germany. This was a peer-to-peer video distribution platform committed to open-source software: It used an open-source file-sharing system and only ran on open-source operating platforms such as Linux (Hadzi 2007, 199; Schneider 2011). Another example of these alternative aggregators was Be The Media, which was run by four UK IndyMedia collectives.[6] It was an aggregator website that collected activist content, including videos from various alternative news outlets, campaign websites, and blogs (Be The Media 2014).

Film and Television Fan Videos

The group of film and television fan video makers that is the subject of this book did not go by a particular name, and is in fact difficult to delineate with any precision. Its roots can be traced to the pioneers of fan video production and distribution from the mid-1970s and to "slash" fandom (Freund 2014, 284). Its members identified it as a predominately female group, and it was geographically dispersed, primarily drawing membership from across the United States, Canada, and Western Europe. Some of my informants from this group were early pioneers and prominent figures of fan video making, while others had only become involved during the Internet era. The group's main focal points, when I initially encountered it in 2011, were the LiveJournal online journaling website, the VividCon fan video convention held annually in Chicago, and the emerging European branch of VividCon, vidUKon, held in the UK. The group started to take on the form that I found it in 2011 at the beginning of the 2000s: VividCon was founded in 2002, and Live-Journal had been widely adopted by 2003 (Coppa 2006, 57). For convenience's sake, the term "the LiveJournal vidding community" is used throughout the remainder of this book as the primary name for this group (following Jenkins (2009, 117–118) and Freund (2014) who also discuss the same group).[7]

The group's genesis, and that of film and television fan video making as a whole, can be traced to 1975 and a slide show set to a fan-made folk song: The slide show was produced by Kandy Fong (one of the original members of the group and an informant for the first phase of the field-work), who used slides produced from cells taken from cutting room floor footage of episodes of *Star Trek: The Original Series* that "went with the song", with the slide changes timed to an audio cassette recording of the song. The slide show was first shown at her local Star Trek fan club, and then at fan conventions across the US (Coppa 2008, 3.1–3.3).

After these early beginnings, the slide show gave way to the videotape as the preferred medium. The video production process typically involved two analogue tape players cabled together, where one would provide the source material and the other would capture the desired clip from the source. These clips would be timed to appear, as with the slide show, during the segment of the song they were chosen to accompany, with the song being dubbed over the original sound track on the destination tape. The process was arduous: It required continual pausing and rewinding of the source tape to find the right frame to start a capture from, precise timings for desired clips and song lyrics, a detailed knowledge of the video players' peculiarities (for example, knowing how many seconds one's particular model rolled back on pause), and access to a library of quality source material. The resulting videos were montages of scenes from different episodes of a particular television series, or sometimes from different television series or films, rearranged to explore a particular theme, decontextualized from the original episodic narrative by both scene selection and the elimination of the original soundtrack, and recontextualized by what was typically a soft rock or pop music song (Bacon-Smith 1992, 175–176; Coppa 2008, 4.2; Jenkins 1992, 225, 244, 247). The choice of song was crucial to the recontextualization of the scene rearrangement and the development of the video's theme, with the lyrics of the song either supporting the visual narrative of the montage or running "counter to it for an ironic or humorous effect" (Bacon-Smith 1992, 177).

One example of this kind of fan video explores the relationship between the characters Tasha Yar and Data in *Star Trek: The Next Generation*. It is a montage of scenes showing their interaction over different episodes with Carole King's song "Tapestry" as the soundtrack, suggesting a much more significant romantic relationship between the two than is actually explicit in the series. While the producers of the series denied that such a relationship existed, fans asserted it nonetheless (Jenkins 1992, 230–231). Another type of early fan video was the "slash" video, which suggested and explored homoerotic relationships between characters that were not explicit, or even present implicitly, in the source material. One example of this type of video suggested a repressed homoerotic relationship between the male leads in *Starsky and Hutch*, set to the song "Leaving the Straight Life Behind" by Jimmy Buffet (Jenkins 1992, 225). Other early fan video types included those that foregrounded secondary characters (for example, Vila in *Blake's 7*), compared television characters to their real world counterparts or fictional characters from other media (the Enterprise crew from *Star Trek: The Original*

Series compared to the crew of Jacques Cousteau's ship Calypso), or reworked the original into another genre (*Star Wars* science fiction genre reworked into crime and romance) (Jenkins 1992, 226–227).

Jenkins summarizes the motivations of these type of video makers and their audiences as follows: "Though made of materials derived from network television, these videos can satisfy fan desires in ways their commercial counterparts all too often fail to do, because they focus on those aspects of the narrative that the community wants to explore" (1992, 249). He theorizes this behaviour using the idea of textual poaching, as expounded by Michel de Certeau, who sees readers of popular fiction as "nomads poaching their way across fields they did not write" (de Certeau 1988, 174). De Certeau, according to Jenkins, sees "popular reading as a series of 'advance and retreats, tactics and games played with the text,' as a type of cultural bricolage through which readers fragment texts and reassemble the broken shards according to their own blueprints, salvaging bits and pieces of the found material in making sense of their own social experience" (Jenkins 1992, 26).

While de Certeau draws a sharp distinction between writers and readers, Jenkins rejects this since, as we have already seen, some fans are both "writers" and "readers" who "do not simply consume preproduced stories; they manufacture their own fanzine stories and novels, art prints, songs, videos, performances etc.... [Fandom] blurs the boundaries between producers and consumers, spectators and participants, the commercial and the homecrafted ... [it] becomes a participatory culture which transforms the experience of media consumption into the production of new texts, indeed of a new culture and a new community" (1992, 45–46). Jenkins expands upon this communal aspect, with specific reference to fan videos, when he says that "the creation, exhibition, and exchange of videos creates the conditions for a communal art form, one contrasting with the commercial culture from which it is derived in its refusal to make a profit and its desire to share its products with others who will value them ... What the videos articulate is what the fans have in common: their shared understandings, their mutual interests, their collective fantasies" (1992, 248–249).

For Jenkins, de Certeau's term "poaching" "forcefully reminds us of the potentially conflicting interests of producers and consumers, writers and readers. It recognizes the power differential between the 'landowners' and the 'poachers'; yet it also acknowledges ways fans may resist legal constraints on their pleasure and challenge attempts to regulate the production and circulation of popular meanings" (1992, 32). This conflict manifested in different ways for pre-Internet fan video producers. For example, fans struggled "with and against the meanings imposed upon them by their borrowed materials" (Jenkins 1992, 33), such as in the examples above asserting particular kinds of relationships between characters that were not explicit in the source material, or even asserting relationships that were directly denied by the producers of that material. This conflict also took on a potentially more threatening form, with fans concerned about being sued for copyright violation by the rights holders of the programmes and music they "poached" from, which led to these videos being distributed within fan communities only, and out of the public eye (Coppa 2008, 1.5; Jenkins 1992, 247, 2009, 117).

Fan videos in the pre-Internet era were distributed on videocassette tapes at conventions and at gatherings in private residences, and typically done person-to-person by the video makers themselves. Conventions and private residences were also the primary venues for the exhibition of these works. Some fan producers also distributed videotapes via post. The producers typically did not charge for their creations, but usually asked the person desiring a copy to provide a blank videotape for duplication (Bacon-Smith 1992, 179; Jenkins 1992, 238–239, 247).

Many scholars argue that fan video culture underwent a major transformation in its move from offline to online, becoming far more widespread, when measured by the number of producers, the number of videos produced, and their audiences' size and diversity. The improvements in production and distribution technology brought about by the digital and Internet eras, liberating producers from the tedium and complexity of analogue home video production and the relatively costly and time-intensive traditional distribution methods, are cited as the primary enablers of this increase (Jenkins 2006a, 135, 137, 2009, 117; Lamerichs 2008, 53; Russo 2009, 125; Strangelove 2010, 114, 118).

The widening of the audience for fan videos from a relatively private group of committed and informed fans to a much more public and diverse one was not unproblematic. For example, Russo (2009) and Ng (2008, 118–119) both discuss issues related to the reception of queer fan videos by wider audiences. Russo considers the example of the fan video "Closer", a *Star Trek: The Original Series* "slash" video featuring the characters Kirk and Spock that appeared on YouTube in 2006 without the maker's permission. She states [following Jenkins (2006b)] that while this video was read within the relevant fan community as a disturbing story about rape, the wider Internet audience saw a camp humour in it: "Concern over the decontextualization of fan vids such as 'Closer' might appear hypocritical because the form itself relies on the possibility of multiple readings and on the selective repurposing of footage. However, what is at issue is not the prerogative of an intended meaning, but the ideological implications of the mutations such meanings can undergo when deracinated" (Russo 2009, 128–129).

Her concern is that videos like "Closer" are being interpreted by the wider audience as being part of a milieu that is dominated by parody videos, such as those concerning the movie *Brokeback Mountain*, which she says often embody homophobic responses to queerness: "A fan vid thrust into this milieu is likely to be read according to these prevailing

conventions, falling into step with values hostile to those of its indige-
nous community" (Russo 2009, 129). However, she also sees a dilemma
here for queer fan video makers: "Without some degree of mainstream-
ing, vidders' rich ecology of queer viewing practices would be relegated
to obscurity, ceding YouTube to gay caricatures. However, we must also
ask what dimensions of this queering are available to be popularized
or commercialized, and, by contrast, what dimensions might be lost or
sidelined ..." (Russo 2009, 129).

This concern about pre-Internet fan video makers' practices being relegated to obscurity and "written out of the history of mashup culture"
(Jenkins 2009, 118) also posed a dilemma for makers of genres other
than slash, who feared a more public profile might attract the unwanted
attention of copyright holders. However, this fear was not restricted to
pre-Internet fan producers weighing the risks of embracing the Internet,
as it also extended to those who had already embraced it, some of whom
continued to maintain relatively limited Internet distribution as a result
(Hill 2009, 174). Some of those desiring to limit their distribution es-
chewed YouTube in favour of video distribution platforms that attracted
less attention, such as iMeem, where access was further restricted by
making the videos only available to those who were their friends on the
platform (Jenkins 2009, 117–118).

While some fan video makers in the Internet era avoided the attention of professional producers and distributors, others courted it. These
video makers exploit the publicness of the Internet to get the attention
of professionals with a view to breaking into the industry. *Star Wars*
parody videos like "Troops" and "George Lucas in Love" appropriated
themes, aesthetics, characters, and even props from professional film
and television in their own video creations, rather than mashing up
existing footage, to create their own industry "calling cards" (Jenkins
2006a, 136, 147).

Another consequence of the transformation of fan video culture from
something shared in private by small, isolated groups to a larger and
more public phenomenon is that these groups came into contact with
each other in the online public spaces they shared, such as YouTube.
This has resulted in the creation of fan videos that borrow from, parody,
and in other ways reflect the fan videos of other fandoms. For example, Michael Strangelove discusses how Chris Crocker's "Leave Britney
Alone" video on YouTube, where a fan of Britney Spears pleads for people
to stop criticizing her, has been remade by fans of Dora the Explorer,
SpongeBob SquarePants, and Star Wars (2010, 114–116).

As we will see in the final section of this chapter, the priorities of an
Internet platform's users do not always align with those of the platform's
owners and operators, and this can lead to problems for users trying to
distribute their videos on them. Coppa (2013, 86) provides an example
of such a situation faced by the fan video makers with regard to iMeem.

We saw above that some of them were attracted to iMeem because of its lower profile as a distribution medium than YouTube, and Coppa (2013, 86) adds that it was also attractive to fans because of its "superior visual quality and audio-visual synchronization ... [and] strong social networking features, allowing fans to friend each other and to create discussion forums, technical-support groups, and thematic playlists". Some time after fan video makers adopted iMeem, it introduced banner ads that were placed over videos, and then it eventually announced that it would no longer host amateur content because it was not sufficiently profitable. Coppa explains that this decision meant that "an entire fan network was disrupted and an archive of fan vids was destroyed; vidders were not even allowed to back up their own videos before they were eliminated" (2013, 86). We will see in Chapter 5 that, unfortunately for the fan video makers, this conflict with iMeem was not an isolated example.

Public Access Television

The California Community Media Exchange (CACMX) was an association of seven community media centres in northern California. These centres consisted of a television station that broadcasted up to three separate channels over the local cable television company's network, whose extent was geographically restricted to the town or county the centre was located in, and some also had a low-power FM radio station. The three channels were a public access channel, which is the subject of this study; an education channel, often run in collaboration with the local school board; and a government channel, which broadcasted local government-related programming.[8]

The public access channels at these centres broadcasted programming produced by local residents (or by people sponsored by local residents), and the charter of the centres was such that there was very little restriction on what could be broadcast, with only programming that had commercial or offensive content being prohibited. The centres also typically provided equipment, facilities, and training to the local residents to help them with the production of their programmes. The centres were non-profit organizations, and their funding came primarily from money granted to them by the councils of the cities that they served, which in turn was mostly derived from fees paid to the city councils by cable television companies in return for permission to operate a cable television franchise within those cities.

The adjective "access" in "public access television" refers to both the access to equipment, facilities, and training mentioned above and to the audience access these centres provide via their channels. The impetus in the US for this idea of providing the public with access to the television screen emerged from both the countercultural movements of the 1960s and from the US constitutional commitment to free speech (Fuller

1994, 4; Rennie 2006, 48). Public access television is seen variously as a medium that gives a voice to people and ideas under-represented or mis-represented in mainstream television programming (Casey and Calvert 2008, 1), that mobilizes "citizens for bringing about social change" (Casey and Calvert 2008, 28), and that builds community (Rennie 2006, 52; Stein 2002, 136).

The genesis of public access television in the US can be traced to two events occurring at the beginning of the 1970s. The first was in 1970 when "two cable [television] franchises were awarded for the borough of Manhattan, with two public access channels ... written into the contract at the last minute. One [franchisee] provided the community with a studio with a camera, a playback deck, and a director free of charge" (Rennie 2006, 50). The second was a year later when the Federal Communications Commission (the US media and communications regulatory body) held hearings into cable television. Provisions coming out of those hearings required cable television network operators to provide local communities free access to facilities for the production and broadcast of their own programming "on a first-come, first-served, non-discriminatory basis" (Fuller 1994, 4–5). This institutionalization of access, underpinned by funding provided by the cable companies and local government, combined with the sheer scale public access television would eventual grow to – involving around 2,000 stations producing more programming than all the major US commercial networks combined – makes it a unique achievement within the genre of community video (Higgins 2007, 185; Linder 1999, 35, 51).

In spite of this apparent success, some believe that the promise of public access television has not been realized. Rennie (2006, 50) argues, for example, that its radical democratic ideal is not reflected in the public access channels' programming schedules, although she admits some examples of this do exist. Fuller (1994, 32–33, 188), while focusing on its success, believes that lack of both funding and audiences has hindered its ability to deliver on its promise in the face of a very competitive commercial television market.

The producers of public access programming are a very diverse group. Linder (1999, 37–38) states that "there is no 'profile' for a public access television producer. The people who use the forum include local activists, senior citizens, elected officials, teenagers, and business people, amongst others. It is impossible to make any generalizations about so varied a group. Perhaps all that can be said about these individuals is that they recognize the value of non-commercial, uncensored television". In addition to individual producers, a diverse array of organizations are also involved in producing shows, including various associations, societies, service providers, and interest groups. Along with this diversity of producers comes a diversity of programming, "which ranges from silly to sublime, serious to sensational" (Linder 1999, 37–38). Fuller (1994, 77–78) provides an extensive list of examples illustrating this diversity, a small selection of which include arts programming, such as Tampa Bay's show on its performing arts centre, programmes advocating social change like the Citizens for Affordable Safe Energy's shows concerning nuclear energy, children's programmes such as the game show "Triviosity" in Massachusetts, and programming from local community groups concerning issues such as AIDS, the environment, and disability.

While it is beyond the scope of this section to provide a detailed analysis of public access television programming, one early example highlights its radical roots, as well as some of the production values commonly associated with it. Paper Tiger Television, a volunteer media collective of artists, activists, academics, and media professionals located in Manhattan, began in 1981 and was broadcast by one of the original public access stations, the Manhattan Neighborhood Network. It has produced hundreds of programmes, with its first programmes involving media theorists critically reading publications such as the *New York Times* and *Vogue*, examining issues such as gatekeeping and agenda setting with the aim of giving viewers a critical understanding of the media (Rennie 2006, 51; Stein 2002, 130). Stein (2002, 130) states that "the collective's strategy is premised on the notion that critical viewers will eventually become assertive citizens who demand that the media be utilized for more democratic purposes". Its basic format of a media theorist in a studio talking were, according to Rennie (2006, 51), often "deliberately rough-edged with hand-drawn graphics cards and visible booms". Similarly, Halleck (2002, 118) describes the aesthetic as "handmade, a comfortable nontechnocratic look that says friendly and low budget. The seams show".

As Linder (1999, 36–37) points out, the facilities, equipment, and support available to producers from the community media centres varies considerably depending on the centres' circumstances: "larger cities … have some of the more sophisticated operations … In smaller cities and rural towns, the extent of the public access operation is more likely to be a camcorder and a playback deck in the office at the local cable company". Typically, though, and this reflects the circumstances of the CACMX centres discussed in Chapter 6, each community media centre has "a studio with two or three cameras mounted on tripods, a switcher, an audio board with inputs for several microphones", along with "field equipment consisting of portable cameras, tripods, light kits, and microphones" and one or more video editing suites. All these are available to use free of charge, and some stations also have salaried staff to train and assist producers in the operation of the facilities and equipment (Linder 1999, 36–37).

Academic studies of Internet use by community media centres and their producers to distribute public access television are scant. The only substantial one, Fuentes-Bautista's (2014) case study of channelAustin, which managed three public access channels in Austin, Texas, does provide some relevant context, however. The programme producers she interviewed used a number of distribution methods in addition to the cable channels, including the producers' own websites, social media platforms, video hosting platforms, as well as offline methods such as festivals and church groups. One example she gives is The Atheist Community, an educational non-profit organization, which produced the show "The Atheist Experience" to help promote its secular viewpoint. Fuentes-Bautista (2014, 73) explains that in addition to being broadcast on a public access channel, episodes of the show were also streamed live over the Internet on the UStream platform and uploaded to three video hosting platforms (Google Video, YouTube, and Blip), where the episodes were archived.[9] The group also engaged with their audience through Facebook, a blog, and a wiki. She reports that in fact "many producers used web-based distribution services … to promote their productions and reach online audiences for their shows", and that there were "many instances in which their contact with audience members [were] facilitated by online tools". For example, social media platforms and email were used to invite audience participation in programme production (Fuentes-Bautista 2014, 75).

Fuentes-Bautista also reports that the producers at channelAustin believed that commercial video distribution platforms like YouTube had several disadvantages relative to cable distribution. These included:

a   Exposure to an audience that is fragmented and non-local. This aspect was seen as a significant disadvantage by producers whose programs are directed to local audiences, as they speak to particular realities of the Austin community;
b   Limited space to store large quantities of quality video;
c   Inability to reach local audiences who do not use computers and lack Internet access; and
d   … the inability to manage and administer copyrights of content distributed over commercial video sharing websites.

(2014, 73)

While the dearth of scholarly studies on public access television's use of the Internet suggests a widening of CACMX's context to include other kinds of online community video, a closer examination of this broader genre shows however that a discussion of it is best left until the next section, which provides a general discussion of the nature of video-based communities online (amongst other things). To see why this is so, we must first address the definition of community media. This is a problematic concept due to the difficulties in defining its parent genre, alternative media, and also due to the elusiveness of the term "community" (Jankowski and Prehn 2002, 5; Rennie 2006, 25).[10] One way the notion of community has been tackled is to distinguish between different forms of community. These can include communities that are characterized by their geographic boundaries, those that are defined by shared interests (communities of interest), and also so-called "virtual" or online communities (Bailey et al. 2008, 8–9; Jankowski and Prehn 2002, 5–6). Since the current concern here is with Internet video only, the distinctions between these different forms blur considerably, however: A group whose members are not defined geographically and who interact online concerning a shared interest are simply a type of online community. What's more, this category of online communities of interest is as relevant to visionOntv and the LiveJournal vidding community as it is to CACMX, as are discussions of online communities in general, and as a result, these two categories will be addressed in the next section. Also, expanding CACMX's context to include the other category of online community media, which is characterized by geographic boundaries, would provide little additional useful context, given the specific history and features of US public access television, and so it will not be addressed here.

Online Video Distribution, Community, and Power

This section moves away from the genre-based approach of the chapter so far and briefly examines two prominent themes emerging from studies of online video in general: the role of online video in community formation and practices and the nature of power relations between users and the video hosting platforms they use. This will provide additional context for each of the groups in the following chapters beyond that provided by the genre discussions so far, enabling these themes to be addressed more thoroughly within them.

Online video and community. Some of the early studies of YouTube focused on the social behaviour of YouTube users and often framed these in terms of the notion of community. For example, Lange (2008), in her study of prominent YouTube amateur producers and their fans, states that some of them saw YouTube as a community. She found that the type of community they described "often moved beyond watery notions of 'feel good togetherness' and would actually cite specific examples of social linkages and related attributes. These included: intensity of shared interests; a willingness to engage in reciprocal acts of kindness both emotionally and financially; and even the inevitable friction and drama that results from community participation. Acts of kindness include assistance that may relate directly to video making as well as activities that focus on helping ill people or people who need financial assistance to attend meet-ups" (Lange 2008, 93).

The meet-ups Lange refers to were actual physical gatherings of fans and YouTube celebrities, showing that online and offline interactions can sometimes be intermingled for video makers and their audiences. Lange (2007) provides other examples of these kinds of online-offline interactions, such as how weak social ties existing between children belonging to an offline support group for the home-schooled were enhanced by their joint production of videos for YouTube and their participation together on it and how latent ties between three dormitory neighbours were activated by their chance involvement in a YouTube video as subjects, on the one hand, and film maker, on the other.

Video blogging, or "vlogging", has been seen as an important aspect of community formation on YouTube, with some arguing it is "fundamental to YouTube's sense of community" and an "emblematic form of YouTube participation" (Burgess and Green 2009a, 94). The co-creative and reciprocal features of many YouTube vlogs underpin their importance in this respect, where they often represent a dialogue over time with other YouTube users, and other vloggers in particular, with different vlog entries incorporating or reflecting the comments, reactions, and criticisms previous entries have garnered (Burgess and Green 2009a, 105; Strangelove 2010, 77). The relationship between vlogging and community on YouTube continues to attract scholarly attention. For example, a recent study (Smith 2016) investigates a vlogging team of two brothers called the VlogBrothers, one of whom is a published author whose ethos of "imagining others more complexly" frames a community called Nerdfighteria, who embrace and propagate this ethos on YouTube through vlogs and discursively through other platforms of the "blogosphere".

Nerdfighteria can be classed as not only a community of vloggers (and bloggers), but also more generally as a community of interest. Examples of communities of interest formed around activities other than vlogging include a study by Light et al. (2012) of a network of graffiti artists on YouTube called Wildstyle. Members of this community provided each other with support and encouragement by, for example, the uploading of "how to" videos by established graffiti artists to assist novice members in their creative development and by other members making encouraging or helpful comments on novices' videos and comments. Light et al. (2012, 249) argue that the community was characterized by "a genuine ethos of a desire to share information, provide support and engage in critique". In another example, Carroll (2008) discusses swing dancers' use of YouTube, where sharing archival footage of swing dance steps, new videos recreating those steps, and videos of recent dance sessions, along with commenting on those videos, are all aspects of community-building practices. For this online community, unlike Nerdfighteria and Wildstyle, the actual activity of dancing itself, within their separate, geographically local communities, was the most important social interaction for the members, not the online interactions.

One final example concerns the communities that form around individual contemporary Christian congregational songs uploaded to YouTube. Thornton and Evans (2016, 143) argue that "the individual song (its lyrics and music as rendered in a popular commercial recording) is the centre of gravity of each virtual community", which makes these communities "quite unique, given that Christian groups/communities/churches have most often historically formed around theological and denomination distinctions". The videos that were part of their study each had millions of views and tens of thousands of likes, comments, and subscribers. Thornton and Evans (2016, 156) found that these communities exhibited many of the traits associated with offline Christian communities, including "intimate communication … as people share vulnerable thoughts and stories allowing the community to (pastoral) care for them via their responses". Unlike offline Christian communities, however, they did not find evidence of deep relationships or a commitment to the community by the members.

While the above examples are just a small sample of the diverse studies concerning the role of online video in community formation and practices, they highlight some of the key aspects of these kinds of social relations, which supplement the context provided by the earlier, genre-based discussions of online video.

Power and social media platforms. Another prominent theme within academic discussions of online video concerns questions of power, and in particular, the power relations between the users of the platforms, on the one hand, and the owners and operators, on the other. One example of the kinds of conflicts that can arise between these two parties comes from the period when YouTube was beginning its commercialization process and concerns the resistance by prominent YouTube producers and their audiences against the launch of Oprah Winfrey's YouTube channel (Brouwers 2008; Burgess and Green 2008, 2009b, 91ff; Strangelove 2010, 111ff). The channel was given special privileges by YouTube's management during its early existence, including the ability to edit the featured video list on YouTube's home page to promote itself, and it also prevented comments from being made on its videos. In response to this "there was an intense and immediate flurry of protest videos, spawning discussion about the implications of this event. One point made by several commentators was that Oprah was importing the convergence of celebrity and control associated with 'big media' into the social media space … and therefore ignoring the cultural norms … of the network" (Burgess and Green 2009b, 91–92), such as the norm that all YouTube users should be treated as equal within its attention economy, and that YouTube participation is an inherently two-way affair. The users' attempts, through these protests, to enforce what they saw as YouTube's norms and preserve, in their eyes, its egalitarian and participatory identity were however ultimately futile in preventing YouTube's owners and operators from developing that platform with a different ethos in mind.

This particular case is just one example of a wider "conflict between the global multimedia business networks that try to commodify [the Internet] and the 'creative audience' that tries to establish a degree of citizen control over it and to declare its right to communicative freedom without corporate control or interference" (Fenton 2012, 127–128).

Some argue that looking to YouTube, for example, as a place to assert this "communicative freedom" in the face of its commodification is a mistake: The assumption that YouTube is "a place to speak one's mind and engage in productive dialogue about salient issues ... is dangerous, [and based on the misplaced belief] that YouTube operates via a model of free speech rather than one of business and capital" (Hess 2009, 426).

Not only does the commodification of platforms like YouTube mean that their ongoing development is guided by a business logic, rather than a participative one, but some also claim that their commodification exploits users. Fuchs (2015), for example, sees this exploitation manifest in various ways, including the fact that the digital labour of the vast majority of users goes unpaid while the owners of the platforms profit from it (such as through the sale of advertising). While it might be argued that users can avoid exploitation by simply not using these platforms in the first place, Fuchs contends that "large platforms such as Facebook have successfully monopolised the supply of certain services, such as online networking ... which allows them to exercise a soft and almost invisible form of coercion, in which users are chained to commercial platforms because all of their friends and important contacts are there" (2015, 229).

Conflict between users and platforms can manifest in other ways, such as when the user comes up against the "commercial infrastructure and rules that undergird distribution sites" (Lange 2017, 150). Lange highlights one common example of this kind of conflict, which arises when YouTube perceives that a video violates copyright law, resulting in the video being taken down, having its sound track removed, or having advertising inserted to monetize the video on behalf of the copyright holder. She reports that this is often done without warning or explanation, and in some cases where the user uploading the video believes it satisfies the "fair use" provisions in copyright law.[11] While users are free to upload to other sites if they find YouTube's terms of services or practices too restrictive, these "other sites might not have adequate traffic ... [and] have their own terms and conditions and commercial pressures that influence what remains online. ... Finding a place of distributive purity online is, admittedly, difficult" (Lange 2017, 150–151).

Conclusion

Placing the three subject producer groups into their historical, pre-Internet context will enable a more comprehensive analysis of the different forms they took, and of the various video distribution practices they engaged in, during the fieldwork than if the context was limited to the Internet era alone. One reason for this, echoing Jenkins (2009, 109), is that while many aspects of Internet video are novel, other aspects have historical precedents, and the historical context developed here will help discern between the two in the ethnography chapters and provide a fuller understanding of these latter dispositions and practices. For example, visionOntv's participatory approach to activist video, and its integration of production, distribution, and exhibition, which will be discussed in detail in Chapter 4, have been shown in this chapter to have precedents in the pre-Internet era of activist video. This historical approach, of course, also provides a framework within which to examine the traditional methods of distribution that continued to be used by the groups alongside the Internet during the periods of this study's fieldwork.

In addition, the observations in this chapter regarding the state of these genres in the Internet era, along with those concerning some of the more general considerations of the last section, will allow for comparisons to be drawn with the experiences of the producers in the subject groups, providing additional insights into their circumstances. For example, some of the general observations reviewed in the last section about the power relationships between users and platforms will help put the specific examples of these discussed in the ethnography chapters into their wider context. This chapter's survey of the issues and themes that emerged from earlier academic studies therefore provided a conceptual framework for both collecting data in the ethnographic field and for the later analysis of these data, although, as we will see in the next chapter, this framework did not adequately capture some crucial aspects of my early encounters in the field, which required the adoption of additional conceptual tools.

Notes

1 Terms such as "pre-Internet era", "Internet era", and "advent of the Internet" are used as shorthand here to distinguish between two historical periods, but are not meant to be taken as precise and well-defined divisions of time: "Pre-Internet era", for example, refers to the period before the advent in the public domain of the Internet as a video distribution technology. This advent, however, did not occur at some specific point in time, nor is the technology one specific thing. Instead, it can be seen as something unfolding over a number of years from the late 1990s (1999 was the earliest date any of the groups studied here reported making their videos available online) to the mid-2000s as different technological changes occurred and were adopted, such as, for example, increased modem transfer rates and the launch of YouTube.

2 It should be noted that the producer groups continued to employ some pre-Internet technologies and practices alongside those related to the Internet during the period of the fieldwork, as we shall see in the following chapter, and so the discussion of these in some cases is of both contemporary and historical relevance.

3 The Joseph Rowntree Reform Trust was an organization that funded "political campaigns in the UK to promote democratic reform, civil liberties and social justice" (Joseph Rowntree Reform Trust Ltd 2013). While Undercurrents had originally considered keeping the project within itself, Rowntree preferred a legal structure that allowed them some formal control over it.

The funding provided to visionOntv was in the form of a one-off grant at the beginning of the project.

4 While the term "activist video" is used throughout this book to describe visionOntv's video output, it should be noted, as Waltz points out, that while activist media encourage their audiences "to get actively involved in social change", they include "media that advocate absolutely mainstream actions, such as voting for the politician of your choice or volunteering for charity" (2005, 3). While the term "radical activist video" (Presence 2015) is sometimes used to limit the category to oppositional and counterhegemonic video, the term "activist video" is used throughout this book for simplicity's sake on the understanding that it refers to this more restricted category.

5 See, for example, Hogenkamp (1986) and Dickinson (1999).

6 The Independent Media Centre, also known as IndyMedia, was a worldwide network of activist media collectives that came into being during the Seattle World Trade Organization protests in 1999 (Downing 2003, 251).

7 It should be noted that using the term "LiveJournal vidding community" elides some complexities. First, there were probably more than one film and television fan video making community on LiveJournal during the two phases of the fieldwork (Freund 2014, 284). The term is used here, however, as shorthand for a more extended set of criteria other than simply being film and television fan video makers who used LiveJournal as the central platform for their fan video activity: The fan producers discussed here also acknowledged VividCon as an important event within their group's annual calendar (and, in fact, all the informants for this book had either attended VividCon or vidUKon). In addition, these producers all identified with the history of the group outlined in this section, and with the same cadre of veteran video makers discussed here and in Chapter 5.

Second, as we will see in Chapter 5, LiveJournal became an increasingly problematic platform for the group, so by the end of the second phase of the fieldwork the name had in fact become a misnomer, and so the group is sometimes simply referred to as the "vidding community" when discussing this stage of their history. It should also be noted here that the terms "vidder" and "vidding" are emic terms used by the informants to describe themselves and their fan video making practices, although these terms are not generally used in this book.

8 For this reason the centres were often also referred to as "PEG stations", although the term "community media centres" is used throughout this book as that was the term preferred by the centres themselves.

9 Her study appears to be based on fieldwork done in 2008, although this is not explicitly stated.

10 For a discussion of the genre of alternative media, see for example Dowmunt (2007, 3) and the other references cited in the first section concerning the definition of activist video.

11 The "fair use" provision of US copyright law allows for the use of copyrighted material without first gaining the copyright owner's permission if the usage satisfies certain criteria. We will examine this in more detail in the following chapters, as this provision, and how it was interpreted, had a significant impact on some of the producer groups. It should be noted though that different legal jurisdictions have different provisions, and in the UK, which is the other main jurisdiction where the groups were active, the provision is known as "fair dealing" and involves a different set of criteria. For the sake of brevity, these provisions will be referred to as "fair use" throughout the book as the specific differences between the jurisdictions are not significant in what follows.

References

Atkinson, Joshua D. 2010. *Alternative Media and Politics of Resistance: A Communication Perspective*. Edited by Lynda Lee Kaid and Bruce Gronbeck, *Frontiers in political communication*. New York: Peter Lang Publishing.

Atton, C. 2002. *Alternative Media*. London: Sage Publications.

Bacon-Smith, C. 1992. *Enterprising Women: Television Fandom and the Creation of Popular Myth*. Philadelphia, PA: University of Pennsylvania Press.

Bailey, O., B. Cammaerts, and N. Carpentier. 2008. *Understanding Alternative Media*. Maidenhead: Open University Press.

Be The Media. 2014. *About*, [cited June 19 2014]. Available from http://bethemedia.org.uk/aboutus.

Brouwers, J. 2008. "YouTube vs. O-Tube." *Cultures of Arts, Science and Technology* no. 1 (1):107–118.

Burgess, Jean, and Joshua Green. 2008. Agency and Controversy in the YouTube Community. In *IR 9.0: Rethinking Communities, Rethinking Place – Association of Internet Researchers Conference*, IT University of Copenhagen, Denmark.

Burgess, Jean, and Joshua Green. 2009a. "The Entrepreneurial Vlogger: Participatory Culture Beyond the Professional-Amateur Divide." In *The YouTube Reader*, edited by Pelle Snickars and Patrick Vonderau, 89–107. Stockholm, Sweden: National Library of Sweden/Wallflower Press.

Burgess, Jean, and Joshua Green. 2009b. *YouTube: Online Video and Participatory Culture*. Cambridge, UK: Polity Press.

Carroll, S. 2008. "The Practical Politics of Step-Stealing and Textual Poaching: YouTube, Audio-Visual Media and Contemporary Swing Dancers Online." *Convergence* no. 14 (2):183–204. doi:10.1177/1354856507087943.

Casey, B., and B. Calvert. 2008. *Television Studies: The Key Concepts*. 2nd ed. Abingdon: Routledge.

Certeau, Michel de. 1988. *The Practice of Everyday Life*. Berkeley: University of California Press.

Coppa, Francesca. 2006. "A Brief History of Media Fandom." In *Fan fiction and fan communities in the age of the Internet: New essays*, edited by K. Hellekson and K. Busse, 41–59. Jefferson, NC: McFarland.

Coppa, Francesca. 2008. "Women, Star Trek, and the Early Development of Fannish Vidding." *Transformative Works and Cultures* no. 1. doi:10.3983/twc.2008.044.

Coppa, Francesca. 2013. "Pop Culture, Fans, and Social Media." In *The Social Media Handbook*, edited by Jeremy Hunsinger and Theresa Senft, 76–92. New York: Routledge.

Costanza-Chock, S. 2008. New Media Activism: Looking beyond the last 5 minutes. http://web.mit.edu/schock/www/docs/new_media_activism.pdf.

Couldry, N., and J. Curran. 2003. "The Paradox of Media Power." In *Contesting Media Power: Alternative Media in a Networked World*, edited by N. Couldry and J. Curran, 3–16. Lanham, MD: Rowman and Littlefield.

Dickinson, Margaret. 1999. *Rogue Reels: Oppositional Film in Britain, 1945–90*. London: British Film Institute.

Dowmunt, T. 2007. "Introduction." In *The Alternative Media Handbook*, edited by Kate Coyer, Tony Dowmunt, and Alan Fountain, 1–12. London: Routledge.

Downing, J.D.H. 2003. "The Independent Media Center Movement and the Anarchist Socialist Tradition." In *Contesting Media Power: Alternative Media in a Networked World*, edited by N. Couldry and J. Curran, 243–257. Lanham, MD: Rowman and Littlefield.

Fenton, N. 2012. "The Internet and Social Networking." In *Misunderstanding the Internet*, edited by J. Curran, N. Fenton, and D. Freedman, 123–148. Abingdon: Routledge.

Fenton, N., and V. Barassi. 2011. "Alternative Media and Social Networking Sites." *The Communication Review* no. 14 (3):179–196. doi:10.1080/10714 421.2011.597245.

Fountain, A. 2007. "Alternative Film, Video and Television 1965–2005." In *The Alternative Media Handbook*, edited by Kate Coyer, Tony Dowmunt, and Alan Fountain, 29–46. London: Routledge.

Freund, Katharina. 2014. "I Thought I Made a Vid, but Then You Told Me That I Didn't: Aesthetics and Boundary Work in the Fan-Vidding Community." In *The Routledge Companion to Remix Studies*, edited by Eduardo Navas, Owen Gallagher, and Xtine Burrough, 283. New York: Routledge.

Fuchs, Christian. 2015. *Culture and Economy in the Age of Social Media*. New York: Routledge.

Fuentes-Bautista, Martha. 2014. "Rethinking Localism in the Broadband Era: A Participatory Community Development Approach." *Government Information Quarterly* no. 31 (1):65–77.

Fuller, L.K. 1994. *Community Television in the United States: A Sourcebook on Public, Educational, and Governmental Access*. Westport, CT: Greenwood Press.

Hadzi, A. 2007. "A2T: Bridging the Digital Divide." In *The Alternative Media Handbook*, edited by Kate Coyer, Tony Dowmunt, and Alan Fountain, 194–205. London: Routledge.

Halleck, DeeDee. 2002. *Hand-Held Visions: The Impossible Possibilities of Community Media*. New York: Fordham University Press.

Harding, T. 1998. "*Viva camcordistas!* Video Activism and the Protest Movement." In *DiY Culture: Party & Protest in Nineties Britain*, edited by George McKay, 79–99. London: Verso.

Heritage, Ruth. 2008. "Video-Activist Citizenship and the Undercurrents Media Project: A British Case-Study in Alternative Media." In *Alternative Media and the Politics of Resistance: Perspectives and Challenges*, edited by M. Pajnik and J.D.H. Downing, 139–161. Ljublana: Peace Institute.

Hess, Aaron. 2009. "Resistance Up in Smoke: Analyzing the Limitations of Deliberation on YouTube." *Critical Studies in Media Communication* no. 26 (5):411–434. doi:10.1080/15295030903325347.

Higgins, J.W. 2007. "'Free Speech' and U.S. Public Access Producers." In *Community Media: International Perspectives*, edited by Linda K. Fuller, 185–196. New York: Palgrave Macmillan.

Hill, Kathryn. 2009. "'Easy to Associate Angsty Lyrics with Buffy': An Introduction to a Participatory Fan Culture." In *Buffy and Angel Conquer the Internet: Essays on Online Fandom*, edited by M Kirby-Diaz, 172–196. Jefferson, NC: McFarland.

Hogenkamp, Bert. 1986. *Deadly Parallels: Film and the Left in Britain, 1929–1939*. London: Lawrence and Wishart.

Howard, Philip N, Aiden Duffy, Deen Freelon, Muzammil M Hussain, Will Mari, and Marwa Maziad. 2011. Opening Closed Regimes: What Was the Role of Social Media during the Arab Spring? *Project on Information Technology & Political Islam.* https://papers.ssrn.com/sol3/papers.cfm?abstract_id= 2595096.

Jankowski, N., and O. Prehn. 2002. *Community Media in the Information Age: Perspectives and Prospects.* Cresskill, NJ: Hampton Press.

Jenkins, H. 1992. *Textual Poachers: Television Fans and Participatory Culture.* New York: Routledge.

Jenkins, H. 2006a. *Convergence Culture.* New York: NYU Press.

Jenkins, H. 2006b. *How to Watch a Fan-Vid,* [cited 14 December 2010]. Available from www.henryjenkins.org/2006/09/how_to_watch_a_fanvid.html.

Jenkins, H. 2009. "What Happened Before YouTube." In *YouTube: Online Video and Participatory Culture,* edited by Jean Burgess and Joshua Green, 109–125. Cambridge, UK: Polity.

Joseph Rowntree Reform Trust Ltd. 2013. *Home.* Joseph Rowntree Reform Trust Ltd, [cited April 22 2013]. Available from http://www.jrrt.org.uk/.

Juhasz, Alexandra. 2008. "Documentary on YouTube: The Failure of the Direct Cinema of the Slogan." In *Re-Thinking Documentary,* edited by Thomas Austin. New York: McGraw Hill.

Kenix, L.J. 2011. *Alternative and Mainstream Media: The Converging Spectrum.* London: Bloomsbury Academic.

Lamerichs, Nicolle. 2008. It's a Small World After All. *Cultures of Arts, Science and Technology* 1 (1):52–71. www.maastrichtuniversity.nl/web/file?uuid=84bea 832-3a88-4a4f-ac69-cf8d1590b4ee&owner=f171341b-cba0-4133-9b9f-931678 d65aed.

Lange, Patricia G. 2007. Fostering Friendship Through Video Production: How Youth Use YouTube to Enrich Local Interaction. Paper read at *Annual Meeting of the International Communication Association,* 27 May, San Francisco, CA.

Lange, Patricia G. 2008. "(Mis)conceptions About YouTube." In *Video Vortex: Responses to YouTube,* edited by Geert Lovink and Sabine Niederer, 87–99. Amsterdam: Institute of Network Cultures.

Lange, Patricia G. 2017. "Participatory Complications in Interactive, Video-Sharing Environments." In *The Routledge Companion to Digital Ethnography,* edited by Larissa Hjorth, Heather Horst, Anne Galloway, and Genevieve Bell, 147–157. New York: Routledge.

Light, Ben, Marie Griffiths, and Siân Lincoln. 2012. "'Connect and Create': Young People, YouTube and Graffiti Communities." *Continuum* no. 26 (3): 343–355.

Linder, Laura R. 1999. *Public Access Television: America's Electronic Soapbox.* Westport, CT: Praeger.

Ng, Eve. 2008. "Reading the Romance of Fan Cultural Production." *Popular Communication* no. 6 (2):103–121. doi:10.1080/15405700701746525.

O'Connor, Paul. 2011. (Co-founder, Undercurrents), in discussion with the author. October 18.

Presence, Steve. 2015. "The Contemporary Landscape of Video-Activism in Britain." In *Marxism and Film Activism: Screening Alternative Worlds,* edited by Ewa Mazierska and Lars Kristensen, 186–212. Oxford: Berghahn Books.

Rennie, E. 2006. *Community Media: A Global Introduction.* Lanham, MD: Rowman & Littlefield Publishers.

Russo, Julie L. 2009. "User-Penetrated Content: Fan Video in the Age of Convergence." *Cinema Journal* no. 48 (4):125–130.

Sandoval, Marisol, and Christian Fuchs. 2010. "Towards a Critical Theory of Alternative Media." *Telematics and Informatics* no. 27 (2):141–150. doi:10. 1016/j.tele.2009.06.011.

Schneider, Florian. 2011. *KEIN,* [cited 20 April, 2017]. Available from www. opendemocracy.net/florian-schneider/kein.

Smith, Daniel R. 2016. "'Imagining Others More Complexly': Celebrity and the Ideology of Fame among YouTube's 'Nerdfighteria'." *Celebrity Studies* no. 7 (3): 339–353.

Stein, Laura. 2002. "Democratic 'Talk', Access Television and Participatory Political Communication." In *Community Media in the Information Age: Perspectives and Prospects,* edited by Nicholas Jankowski and Ole Prehn, 121–140. Cresskill, NJ: Hampton Press.

Strangelove, Michael. 2010. *Watching YouTube.* Toronto: University of Toronto Press.

Thomas, Peter. 2012. "The British Workshop Movement and Amber Film." *Studies in European Cinema* no. 8 (3):195–209.

Thornton, Daniel, and Mark Evans. 2016. "YouTube: A New Mediator of Christian Community." In *Congregational Music-Making and Community in a Mediated Age,* edited by Anna Nekola and Tom Wagner, 141–160. Abingdon: Routledge.

Uldam, Julie, and Tina Askanius. 2013. "Online Civic Cultures? Debating Climate Change Activism on YouTube." *International Journal of Communication* no. 7:1185–1204.

Undercurrents. 2017a. *About,* [cited April 12 2017]. Available from www.under currents.org/about.html.

Undercurrents. 2017b. *Undercurrents Alternative News Video,* [cited April 12 2017]. Available from www.undercurrents.org/altvideos.html.

Waltz, M. 2005. *Alternative and Activist Media.* Edinburgh: Edinburgh University Press.

3 Assemblages and Actor-Networks

My initial entry into the ethnographic field was framed by the literature reviewed in Chapter 2, which was, as we saw, primarily humanistic in nature, focusing on the social and political interactions between people and organizations engaged in the production, distribution, and consumption of video. Also, the element of the literature concerning online video that was available prior to this initial entry in 2011 was predominantly concerned with YouTube (and mostly remains so, as we saw). After around three months in the field, however, it became clear that the framework provided by this literature could not adequately account for major aspects of what was being encountered in the field. One such aspect was that individual informants were typically using multiple technologies to distribute their videos, either in addition to or instead of YouTube, and the selection and arrangement of the particular mix of these technologies were often complex and problematic processes. In addition, these arrangements were often unstable, with different elements sometimes becoming detached, new ones becoming attached, and sometimes the whole arrangement simply came apart. Finally, the literature's primary focus on the human actors in online video distribution and the relationships between them seemed too narrow: The different technologies used by this study's informants also appeared to be important actors, not simply passive tools, and giving a full account of them, and of the relationships between them and the human actors, was critical to gaining a proper understanding of what was being encountered in the field. I later returned to the field with the concepts of assemblages and actor-networks as the primary theoretical foci, and we will see in the ethnographies that follow this chapter that these concepts provide a framework for capturing and analysing these aspects of online video in considerable detail.

The first section of this chapter provides an outline of Assemblage Theory as formulated by Manuel DeLanda from his reading of Gilles Deleuze and Felix Guattari's concept of assemblages. It is based primarily on DeLanda's (2006b) work that uses Assemblage Theory to develop a social ontology, although the section also draws upon other works by DeLanda, as well as upon those of other theorists, including Deleuze and

Guattari themselves, to clarify, illustrate, and supplement the discussion as required. Beyond this exegesis, the section also examines critiques of Assemblage Theory, as well as exploring some of the different ways it has been employed by scholars to understand digital media. The second section provides an outline of Actor-Network Theory (ANT), drawing upon a broad range of theorist working in the area, and it similarly looks at its critics and at those that have applied it as a framework for analysing digital media. The reason that two conceptual frameworks are used to analyse the ethnographies in the following chapters, rather than just one, comes from an empirical rather than a theoretical motivation: During the fieldwork, it became apparent that while there was overlap between the two frameworks, the theoretical vocabulary, sensibilities, or perspective of one approach would often provide a more faithful rendering of a particular situation than the other. The third and final section of this chapter explores the relationship between these two frameworks, focusing on the implications this has for their application in the chapters that follow.

Assemblage Theory

DeLanda adopts Deleuze's concept of assemblages as a way of addressing what he sees as the fundamental philosophical problem of social ontology: Accounting for the relationship between the macro and the micro levels of social activity (DeLanda 2006a, 250). In tackling this question, he asks: "Is there ... such a thing as society as a whole? ... Is denying the reality of such an entity equivalent to a commitment to the existence of only individual persons and their families?" (DeLanda 2006b, 8). He rejects both the macroreductionism and the microreductionism implicit in these questions, and instead develops an alternative response based on the concept of assemblages.

In developing this alternative, DeLanda first takes aim at what he sees as the main theoretical alternative to an assemblage approach: The entrenched, age-old, macroreductionist social ontology centred on the "organismic metaphor". DeLanda argues that this metaphor, in its basic form, sees the human body as an analogy for society, postulating that "just as bodily organs work together for the organism as a whole, so the function of social institutions is to work in harmony for the benefit of society" (2006b, 8). While this functionalist version of the metaphor has fallen out of favour, DeLanda argues another version continues to persist and remains influential within the social sciences: "This version involves ... a general theory about the relations between parts and wholes, wholes that constitute a seamless totality or that display an organic unity. The basic concept in this theory is what we may call *relations of interiority*: the component parts are constituted by the very relations they have to other parts in the whole. A part detached from such a whole ceases to be what it is, since being this particular part is one of its constitutive properties" (DeLanda 2006b, 9).

On this view, not only do parts that become detached from organic wholes lose their identity, but organic wholes can only be made up of such parts: "A whole in which the component parts are self-subsistent and their relations are external to each other does not possess an organic unity" (DeLanda 2006b, 9). If such wholes do appear unified in some respects, this arises from them being merely mixtures or aggregations. Also, these kinds of wholes do not possess emergent properties, and whatever properties they do have are simply an aggregation of the properties of their components because these components lack relations of interiority (DeLanda 2006b, 9–10).

DeLanda challenges the concept of the relations of interiority that underpins this social ontology:

> We can distinguish, for example, the properties defining a given entity from its capacities to interact with other entities. While its properties are given and may be denumerable as a closed list, its capacities are not given – they may go unexercised if no entity suitable for interaction is around – and form a potentially open list, since there is no way to tell in advance in what way a given entity may affect or be affected by innumerable other entities. ... And given that an unexercised capacity does not affect what a component is, a part may be detached from the whole while preserving its identity.
>
> (2006b, 10)

DeLanda sees Deleuze's concept of assemblages as the main theoretical alternative to the notion of organic wholes, since they are wholes constituted by relations of exteriority rather than by relations of interiority. He states that relations of exteriority imply "a component part of an assemblage may be detached from it and plugged into a different assemblage in which its interactions are different ... In other words, the exteriority of relations implies a certain autonomy for the terms they relate" (DeLanda 2006b, 10). For Deleuze, the idea of relations of exteriority is not a philosophical first principle, but something that arises out of the insights of the empiricist philosophers: "What is it that the empiricists found, not in their heads, but in the world ...? ... *Relations are external to their terms.* 'Peter is smaller than Paul', 'The glass is on the table': relation is neither internal to one of the terms ... nor to two together. Moreover, a relation may change without the terms changing. ... The ideas of the glass and the table, which are the true terms of the relations, are not altered [when the glass is moved off the table]. Relations are in the middle, and exist as such" (Deleuze and Parnet 2006, 41).

The fact that assemblages are wholes consisting of autonomous parts does not prevent them however from having emergent properties, that is, properties not reducible to the properties of their component parts.[1] Deleuze nonetheless emphasizes that these properties are the result of "liaisons", "alliances", and "alloys" of the component parts and that "the assemblage's only unity is that of co-functioning" component parts, which are in a symbiotic relationship with each other (Deleuze and Parnet 2006, 52). According to DeLanda, the reason that assemblages can have emergent properties, yet still be characterized by relations of exteriority, is due to the fact that the properties of an assemblage are "the result not of an aggregation of the components' own properties but of the actual exercise of their capacities. These capacities do depend on a component's properties but cannot be reduced to them since they involve reference to the properties of other interacting entities. Relations of exteriority guarantee that assemblages may be taken apart while at the same time allowing that the interactions between parts may result in a true synthesis" (2006b, 11). Jane Bennett also stresses that the emergent properties of an assemblage are not simply aggregates of its components' properties when she states that "the effects generated by an assemblage are ... emergent properties, emergent in that their ability to make something happen ... is distinct from the sum of the vital force of each [material component] considered alone. Each member and proto-member of the assemblage has a certain vital force, but there is also an effectivity proper to the grouping as such: an agency *of* the assemblage" (2009, 24).

Even though these emergent properties are not reducible to their components' properties, they are imminent and not transcendent: "Because of [the] bottom-up causality [of the component parts] the emergent properties and capacities of a whole are immanent, that is, they are irreducible to its parts but do not transcend them, in the sense that if the parts stop interacting the whole itself ceases to exist, or becomes a mere aggregation of elements" (DeLanda 2010, 68–69). DeLanda illustrates the concept of emergent properties by contrasting the different types of biological examples used by the proponents of the two theories: "While those favouring the interiority of relations tend to use organisms as their prime example, Deleuze gravitates towards other kinds of biological illustrations, such as the symbiosis of plants and pollinating insects. In this case we have relations of exteriority between self-subsistent components – such as the wasp and the orchid" (2006b, 11).

The example of the wasp and the orchid illustrates both how emergent properties of assemblages arise and also the relational characteristic of a component's capacities. The properties of wasps (e.g. having wings) and orchids (e.g. having certain colours, shapes, and odours) give them certain capacities (e.g. transport pollen, attract wasps) that only become apparent upon their interaction. Capacities can therefore be seen as a relational characteristic of a component, unlike its properties: "We may have exhaustive knowledge about an individual's properties and yet, not having observed it in interaction with other individuals, know nothing about its capacities" (DeLanda 2005, 72). The interaction of these capacities in this example gives the wasp-orchid assemblage the emergent property of being an orchid pollinator. This example also illustrates a point made by Wise, paraphrasing Deleuze and Guattari: "we do not know what an assemblage *is* until we can find out what it *can do* ..., that is, how it functions" (2005, 78). The existence of emergent properties is a defining feature of assemblages for DeLanda because "without something ensuring the irreducibility of an assemblage, the concept would not be able to replace that of a seamless totality. If the [properties] of a whole are reducible, then they form an aggregate in which the components merely coexist without generating a new entity" (2016, 12).

DeLanda (2016, 10–11) illustrates how emergent properties and relations of exteriority manifest in social contexts, which will be one of our concerns in the following chapters, through an examination of interpersonal networks of the kind that exist in "tightly knit communities that inhabit small towns" or in "neighbourhoods with an ethnic composition in large cities". For these networks, "an important emergent property is the degree to which their members are linked together", that is, "the *density* of its connections". Dense interpersonal networks are able to rapidly transmit "violation of a local norm", such as "an unreciprocated favour" or "an unpaid bet", the memory of which is stored within the community as part of the transgressor's reputation "to the extent that this information is remembered by enough neighbours", who enforce the norm through "ridicule and ostracism" (DeLanda 2016, 10–11). Density in this context is an "intensive property" of the assemblage: DeLanda defines these as properties that can undergo qualitative changes through an increase in quantity (2016, 76). In this case, insufficiently dense interpersonal networks will not have the capabilities just described, but they may acquire them as more members become linked together.

DeLanda goes on to argue that "the property of density, and the capacity to store reputations and enforce norms, are non-reducible properties and capacities of the entire community, but neither involves thinking of it as a seamless totality in which the very personal identity of the members is created by their relations: neighbours can pack their things and move to a different community while keeping their identity intact" (2016, 12). That is, "with these two concepts – emergence and exteriority – we can define social wholes, like interpersonal networks ..., that cannot be reduced to the persons that compose them, but that do not totalise them either, fusing them into a seamless whole in which their individuality is lost" (DeLanda 2016, 12).

Beyond relations of exteriority and emergent properties, DeLanda identifies three other defining features of assemblages. He sees these features as the "dimensions" or "axes" of an assemblage. One defines the roles played by components in an assemblage, and the other two concern processes that stabilize and destabilize assemblages. The roles defined by the first dimension range "from a purely material role at one extreme of the axis, to a purely expressive role at the other extreme". In addition to these pure roles, "a given component may play a mixture of material and expressive roles by exercising different sets of capacities" (DeLanda 2006b, 12).

One example DeLanda gives to illustrate this first dimension concerns the composition of institutional organizations. Component parts with a material role to play include human bodies, food, physical labour, simple tools, complex machines, and the buildings and neighbourhoods serving as their physical locales. Component parts with an expressive role to play include not only language and symbols, but also bodies through their posture, dress, facial expressions, and behaviours, such as a subordinate obeying a command in public expresses acceptance of the other's authority (2006b, 12–13). The identification of the human body as a component with both a material and an expressive role in this example illustrates how a component can play a mixture of roles within an assemblage: The human body has both the capacity to engage in material activities, such as using a tool, as well as the capacity to be expressive, such as nodding in agreement.

Another example DeLanda gives is of interpersonal networks and communities, where the material components include the constant labour required to maintain the links within these assemblages: "This labour goes beyond the task of staying in touch with others via frequent routine conversations. It may also involve listening to problems and giving advice in difficult situations as well as giving a variety of forms of physical help, such as taking care of other people's children" (2006a, 256). The expressive components in these kinds of networks and communities include: "The variety of expressions of solidarity and trust which emerge from, and then shape, interaction. These range from routine acts, such as having dinner together or going to church, to the sharing of adversity, or the displayed willingness to make sacrifices for the community. Expressions of solidarity may, of course, involve language, but in this case (as in many others) actions speak louder than words" (DeLanda 2006a, 256–257).

DeLanda states that the second of his dimensions for an assemblage "defines variable processes in which these components become involved and that either stabilize the identity of an assemblage, by increasing its degree of internal homogeneity or the degree of sharpness of its boundaries, or destabilize it. The former are referred to as processes of territorialization and the latter as processes of deterritorialization" (2006b, 12). For DeLanda, processes of territorialization are, in the first place, processes that literally "define or sharpen boundaries of actual territories". Continuing with the example of institutional organizations above, he illustrates this aspect of the territorialization process by saying that organizations are involved in providing spatial boundaries: They "usually operate in particular buildings, and the jurisdiction of their legitimate authority usually coincides with the physical boundaries of those buildings". While he admits governmental organizations' spatial boundaries are not typically restricted to particular buildings, their jurisdictions are also usually defined territorially (by international borders, for example) (DeLanda 2006b, 13).

The non-spatial aspect of territorialization processes for DeLanda concerns "the degree to which an assemblage's component parts are drawn from a homogenous repertoire, or the degree to which an assemblage homogenizes its own components" (2010, 13). Such territorializing processes include, for example, "sorting processes which exclude a certain category of people from membership of an organization, or the segregation processes which increase the ethnic or racial homogeneity of a neighbourhood" (DeLanda 2006b, 13). DeLanda's example of how the US computer manufacturing industry is stabilized through a series of non-spatial territorialization processes provides a detailed illustration of these kinds of processes in action:

> The integrating and regulating activities of organizations such as trade and industry associations are a key component of these processes. Industry associations are instrumental in leading their members towards consensus on many normative questions which affect them collectively, particularly the setting of industry-wide technological standards. Trade associations can serve as clearing-houses for information about an industry's sales, prices and costs, allowing their members to coordinate some of their activities. They also reduce interorganizational variation by sponsoring research (the results of which are shared among members) and promoting product-definition and product-quality guidelines. The degree of organizational uniformity is also increased by the creation of behavioural norms by professional and worker associations: norms that may be informal and nonenforceable but which nevertheless help to standardize occupational behaviour, expectations and wages.
>
> (2006b, 82)

The opposite process, deterritorialization, is "any process which either destabilizes spatial boundaries or increases internal heterogeneity" (DeLanda 2006b, 13). Continuing the computer industry example, DeLanda illustrates the non-spatial aspect of this process: "an important deterritorializing factor ... is a turbulent environment, such as that created by a high rate of innovation in products or processes" whereby heterogeneity is introduced into the industry through the different rates the component organizations adapt to these innovations (2006b, 82). An example of the spatial version of this process comes from the role communication technologies, such as telephones or computers, play in social relations: These technologies "blur the spatial boundaries of social entities by eliminating the need for co-presence" (DeLanda 2006b, 13).

DeLanda's treatment of homogeneity and heterogeneity with respect to assemblages differs from that of Deleuze. For Deleuze, heterogeneity is a defining feature of an assemblage (see, for example, Deleuze and Parnet 2006, 52), but DeLanda instead treats it not "as a constant property of assemblages but as a variable that may take different values" (DeLanda 2006b, 12). The computer industry example illustrates this by showing how processes of territorialization, which attempt to homogenize the players in the industry, respond to and contest with deterritorialization processes that increase the heterogeneity of the industry assemblage, and as a result the degree to which the assemblage is heterogeneous varies over time.

A distinction is also made here between two types of deterritorialization, relative and absolute (DeLanda 2006b, 123; Patton 2010, 52). Before explaining the difference between these, it is first necessary to introduce the concept of diagrams, which is another of the defining characteristics of assemblages for DeLanda. A diagram of an assemblage can be thought of as a virtual space that defines the different possible forms a particular type of assemblage may take. These possible forms are points within the diagram, called universal singularities. The position of a universal singularity within this virtual space is defined by the axes of the space, which represent the different characteristics that specify the identities of the particular kinds of assemblages that the diagram represents. An actual assemblage that manifests one of these possible forms in history is called an individual singularity (DeLanda 2006b, 30, 2011, Appendix).

To illustrate the assemblage diagram concept, DeLanda uses Max Weber's classification of authority structures within hierarchical organizations: "There are three different ways in which their authority may gain legitimacy: by reference to a sacred tradition or custom (as in organized religion); by complying with rational-legal procedures (as in bureaucracies); or by the sheer presence of a charismatic leader (as in small religious sects)" (2006b, 30). From these three ways, a set of characteristics for organizational authority can be derived, which would include, for example, "the degree to which an office or position in a hierarchy is clearly separated from the incumbent – rational-legal forms have the most separation, followed by the traditional and charismatic forms – and the degree to which the activities of the organization are routinized – the charismatic form would have the least degree of routinization, while the other two would be highly routinized" (DeLanda 2006b, 31). This set of variable characteristics can then serve as the axes of a diagram for assemblages that are hierarchical organizations, with these axes defining the virtual space of possible assemblages, which are the universal singularities of that space exhibiting the different potential combinations of these characteristics.

It should be noted however that these diagrams are not transcendent, like ideal types or Platonic forms, but rather they are immanent (DeLanda 2016, 115). This is because "in addition to properties, assemblages also possess dispositions, tendencies and capacities that are virtual (real but not actual) when not being currently manifested or exercised" (DeLanda 2016, 108), and it is the potential ways that these can manifest, and the actual historical manifestations of them, within the limits of the characteristics that form the axes of the relevant diagram, that define the diagram's singularities. Assemblages can therefore be "thought as parts of populations in which their identities can change within limits producing a certain statistical distribution of variation" (DeLanda 2011, Appendix).

Returning now to the two types of deterritorialization, a relative deterritorialization process is one that destabilizes the identity of an assemblage to the point where a new territorialization process, called reterritorialization, attempts to reform it with another identity (DeLanda 2006b, 123).[2] These processes can be described within the assemblage diagram: While the actual assemblage, being a singular individual representing an instantiation of a universal singularity on the diagram, has its identity destabilized by the deterritorialization process, the reterritorialization process reforms the identity of the assemblage, with this new identity corresponding to one of the universal singularities defined by the assemblage diagram. Absolute deterritorialization, on the other hand, "involves a much more radical identity change: indeed, a loss of identity altogether, but without falling into an undifferentiated chaos" (DeLanda 2006b, 124). In this case, the assemblage would no longer correspond to any of the universal singularities on the diagram, and therefore would cease to be described by it.

Finally, the third dimension describes another synthetic process that complements territorialization and further helps to stabilize the identity of an assemblage. DeLanda refers to this process as "coding" and its counter-process as "decoding": "Coding refers to the role played by language in fixing the identity of a social whole. In institutional organizations, for example, the legitimacy of an authority structure is in most cases related to linguistically coded rituals and regulations ... in those governed by a rational-legal form of authority they will be written rules, standard procedures, and most importantly, a constitutional charter defining its rights and obligations" (DeLanda 2010, 13).[3] Another example DeLanda uses is conversations. These involve rules, such as turn-taking, and "the more formal and rigid the rules, the more these social encounters may be said to be coded. But in some circumstances these rules may be weakened giving rise to assemblages in which the participants have more room to express their convictions and their own personal styles" (DeLanda 2006b, 16). An illustration of such a decoded conversation according to DeLanda would be an informal one between friends.

A further example DeLanda gives is of coded and decoded software applications, and while not about "social wholes", it helps to further elaborate the concepts at hand.[4] Applications written in old programming languages like Pascal relied on a master program that would stay in control of the computation process notwithstanding temporary surrender of control to subroutines. In contrast to these coded applications, modern "object-orientated" programming languages can write decoded applications, where in place of a master program are a population of autonomous and flexible software objects (DeLanda 2011, Appendix).

DeLanda combines the three dimensions discussed above to characterize an assemblage as a concept with "material and expressive variables and ... territorialization and coding parameters" (2016, 137). He sometimes refers to the concept of assemblages as "a concept with knobs", drawing an analogy between the "actual knobs in a piece of laboratory equipment (knobs which may be tuned to change an artificial phenomenon's environment)" and the parameters of an assemblage (2016, 23). Therefore, for example, an assemblage with these parameters, or "knobs", both set to a high value would be a highly territorialized and highly coded assemblage, such as an authoritarian state with a rigid set of laws and behavioural codes and with a homogenous population or a sharply defined territorial boundary.[5]

The final aspect of assemblages to be addressed here returns to the question posed at the beginning of this section concerning the relationship between the micro and macro levels of social activity. For DeLanda, "each differently scaled individual entity (individual persons, individual organisations, individual cities and so on) is made out of entities at the immediate lower scale, that is, ... the relations among scales is one of parts to whole" (2006a, 251). For DeLanda, this approach relativizes the concepts of "micro" and "macro", making them dependent on the spatial scale under consideration: "organisations, for example, are macro if we are considering persons, but micro if we are considering cities" (2006a, 252).[6] He goes on to state that "each of the singular, individual entities that make up each scale may be considered an assemblage" (2006a, 252). DeLanda illustrates this aspect of his theory using the example of a nomadic army of horse archers: "An army ... should be viewed as an *assemblage of assemblages*, that is, as an entity produced by the recursive application of the part-to-whole relation: a nomad army is composed of many interacting cavalry teams, themselves composed of human-horse-bow assemblages, in turn made out of human, animal and technical components" (2010, 68).

That is, at one scale the cavalry teams, for example, can be considered micro assemblages: They are components that go into making up the nomad army macro assemblage. But considered at another scale, the cavalry teams are macro assemblages, composed of human-horse-bow micro assemblages. DeLanda goes on to argue that at any given scale within such an assemblage of assemblages there are top-down causal effects from the macro assemblage onto the micro assemblages that are its components, and also bottom-up effects from the micro assemblages onto the macro assemblage. DeLanda also uses the nomad army example to explain these causal effects between wholes and parts. With respect to the bottom-up effects, "the properties and capacities of a whole emerge from the causal interactions between its parts: many human-horse-bow assemblages, trained intensively to work together, form a whole with the emergent capacity to take advantage of spatial features of the battlefield, for ambush and surprise, and to exploit temporal features of the battle, such as the fleeting tactical opportunity presented by a temporary break in an enemy's formation" (DeLanda 2010, 68). An assemblage's top-down effect has the capacity to influences how its components operate, constraining some of their capacities while enabling others: "Belonging to a team of warriors makes its members subject to mutual policing: any loss of nerve or display of weakness by one member will be noticed by the rest of the team and affect his or her reputation. But the team also creates resources for its members, as they compensate for each other's weaknesses and amplify each other's strengths" (DeLanda 2010, 69).

It should be clear from the discussion of assemblages in this section so far that there is a dynamic aspect to the concept. This dynamic aspect is in fact present within the original French word used by Deleuze and Guattari, *agencement*, although it is somewhat lost in the conventional translation of that word into English as "assemblage": The French word has both an active sense – "a way of assembling or arranging" – and a passive sense – the resulting "ordering or arrangement" (Deleuze and Parnet 2006, x).[7] Phillips elaborates on these two senses: "*Agencement* is a common French word with the senses of either 'arrangement', 'fitting' or 'fixing' and is used in French in as many contexts as those words are used in English: ... one might talk of fixing (fitting or affixing) two or more parts together; and one might use the term for both the act of fixing and the arrangement itself, as in the fixtures and fittings of a building or shop, or the parts of a machine" (2006, 108). John Law emphasizes the active sense of the word in Deleuze's philosophy when he states that an assemblage is an "uncertain and unfolding process ... a tentative and hesitant unfolding ... It needs to be understood as a verb as well as a noun" (2004, 41–42). DeLanda similarly states that "the identity of any assemblage ... is always the product of a process ... and it is always precarious, since other processes ... can destabilize it" (2006b, 28).

With the overview of Assemblage Theory now complete, we turn to review some of the ways scholars have applied both Deleuze and Guattari's and DeLanda's thinking on assemblages to understanding digital media.[8] The purpose of this review is, first, to show that assemblage concepts can and have been successfully applied to help understand a wide range of digital media and their uses, including online video.

Second, the review will also highlight some specific ways assemblage concepts have been employed in this regard, providing some additional context for the ethnographic chapters that follow as well as providing some specific examples of this usage that will be compared with the findings from those chapters.

Salovaara uses DeLandian Assemblage Theory concepts to argue that political movements such as Pussy Riot are "social assemblages". She sees groups like these as assemblages that "combine urban (material) space via demonstrations, protests and performances, and virtual ecosystems via digital platforms, news flows, hashtags, and memes" (Salovaara 2015, 13). She argues that "agency [within these assemblages] is a distributed phenomenon that can only be understood by tracing the complex ecologies that are distinctive to the topological structure of digital media ecosystems" (Salovaara 2015, 13–14). In another example, Rizzo, drawing on Deleuze and DeLanda amongst others, argues that "multiplatform television is an assemblage that is constantly forming new connections between viewers, texts, technologies, policies and practices ... that shoot off into different directions, are sometimes temporary, and as a consequence form ... assemblages that are open and susceptible to change" (2015, 113–114). She contrasts this with broadcast television, which she sees as highly territorialized (both spatially and in terms of the homogeneity of its components) and coded. Also, Langlois argues that online participatory systems can be understood as assemblages of "elements, actors and processes that are shaped and 'fixed' to 'fit' together ... in order to produce a culturally stable form of communication" (2013, 93). She sees this as having critical value since it "makes it possible to identify processes of governance that articulate one element, process or actor (human or technological) to another, and that reshape these elements, processes, and actors in order to create this stable fit" (Langlois 2013, 93). By "governance", Langlois means "the ensemble of techniques and procedures" that regulate the behaviour of the various actors (2013, 99).

Assemblage thinking has also been used, for example, to analyse computer games (Cremin 2016; De Paoli and Kerr 2009; Taylor 2009), mobile media devices (Wise 2005, 2012), selfies (Hess 2015), the use of live streaming video in relation to contemporary resistance movements (Lenzner 2014; Thorburn 2014), video "witnessing" (Frosh and Pinchevski 2014), how the human component is constituted within the Internet (Savat 2010), the topology of the Internet (Sampson 2007), cultural memory-making through social networks (Tan 2013), and scholarly video production and distribution (Reid 2010).

The final part of this section looks at some critiques of DeLanda's approach to assemblages. The first of these concerns Bueger's criticism of DeLanda's treatment of Deleuze and Guatarri's work on assemblages as an invitation to "contemplate ontological concepts and metaphors", arguing instead that "assemblage thinking is an invitation for empirical work", whose concepts are "rules of thumb" that "have to be defined in empirical work" rather than theoretically (2014, 65). Even if this criticism is accepted, it is met in this book by an inclusive stance: DeLanda's simplification and codification of assemblage thinking is adopted here because it helps facilitate the systematic application of this approach across three detailed empirical case studies, something that would be more difficult to do using the scattered, complex, and very abstract arguments of Deleuze and Guattari alone. This does not imply a slavish implementation of DeLanda though, since the analysis in the following chapters will adapt his concepts as defined above to the empirical context, where they will also be brought into dialogue with the concepts of ANT.

Buchanan is also critical of DeLanda's understanding of Deleuze and Guattari, arguing that his reading of their concept of assemblages is in "error" (2015, 382). His criticism is based primarily on one example of DeLanda's and does not engage with DeLanda's extensive exegesis of Deleuze and Guatarri's work, or with DeLanda's general conceptual framework. However, even if we accept Buchanan's narrowly based criticism (the details of which are not relevant here), DeLanda anticipates such charges pointing out that he uses a reconstruction of Deleuzian ontology and that "Readers who feel that the theory developed here is not strictly speaking Deleuze's own are welcome to call it 'neo-assemblage theory' ... or some other name" (2006b, 3–4). DeLanda's status as a Deleuzian purist is also not a concern for this book, as it makes no claim to be a Deleuzian study, but rather it is one that adopts assemblage and actor-network concepts from different sources to analyse various empirical situations.

A final criticism, coming from Harman, argues that Assemblage Theory is too focused on the instability of assemblages. While he commends Assemblage Theory for challenging theories that treat the world in a static way, he argues that in practice assemblages "also withstand blows and resist reduction" and are only typically subject to "intermittent crisis" (Harman 2014, 128–129). Whether this is a shortcoming of the theory or not, the way it has been applied to the ethnographies that follow does not assume that the assemblages discussed within them are in perpetual crisis or flux. We will see, however, that when they are stable, this is not a given but something that usually requires regular processes of stabilization to maintain, although this is not a top-down theoretically driven principle, but rather a feature of the contingent, empirical situation encountered in the field.

Actor-Network Theory

Bruno Latour traces the origins of ANT to the need for a social theory that was compatible with science and technology studies (2005, 10). One of the earliest papers concerning this new social theory, co-authored by Michel Callon and Latour in 1981, states its defining principle as follows: "What then is a sociologist? Someone who studies associations and dissociations, that is all, as the word 'social' itself implies" (1981, 300). Callon and Latour's formulation of sociology as something that only concerns itself with associations is meant as a challenge to what they see as the conventional understanding of sociology and is proposed as an alternative to it.

Latour claims this conventional understanding "posit[s] the existence of a specific sort of phenomenon variously called 'society', 'social order', 'social practice', 'social dimension', or 'social structure'" (2005, 3). He argues that this phenomenon operates in sociological theory as a domain of reality separate from others, such as, for example, those of science, law, and politics, and is used to explain the "social aspects" of these other domains through "an appeal to social factors" (Latour 2005, 3). For example, while science is a domain of its own, "some features of its quest are necessarily 'bound' by the 'social limitations' of scientists who are 'embedded in the social context of their time'" (Latour 2005, 3). On this view, according to Latour, society is the context that frames all the other domains of human activity (2005, 4). It is an aggregate where people are held together in durable relationships with each other through "social ties". Elaborating on this notion of social ties, Latour states that typically in sociology, "'social' designates a type of link: it's … a sort of material like straw, mud, string, wood, or steel. In principle, you could walk into some imaginary supermarket and point at a shelf full of 'social ties'" (2005, 64).

ANT, as an alternative to this "sociology of the social", as Latour sometimes calls the conventional view, rejects these key elements. For ANT, the social does not exist as a separate domain of reality: There is no overarching social explanatory context for other domains, and there are no such things as social ties in the sense of being durable connections between people. In short, according to Latour, there is no such thing as "society" (2005, 4–5, 9, 64–65). While ANT is a "sociology of associations" rather than one of the "social", the 1981 paper also makes it clear that these associations are not only between humans, but also include non-humans: "For a long time now associations between men have been expanded and extended through other allies: words, rituals, iron, wood, seeds and rain" (Callon and Latour 1981, 300). Three studies published a few years after this initial 1981 formulation, which are considered by Latour to be the seminal works of ANT (2005, 10), foreground the role of non-humans in their narratives and include such things as navigational technology (Law 1986), scallop larvae collectors (Callon 1986), and microbes (Latour 1988a) in the various associations these studies discuss.

Before examining ANT in detail, it is important to note that, in spite of its name, ANT is not a single, cohesive theory. As Latour points out, since these early studies, ANT "has moved in many directions" (2005, 10). Similarly, Law emphasizes that ANT is a kind of "'diaspora' that overlaps with other intellectual traditions" (2009, 141–142), and one that has changed over time as it has been adopted and adapted by different scholars in different intellectual centres (2003, 4). Not only does Law question ANT's status as a single theory, he also questions whether it is a theory at all: "Theories usually try to explain why something happens, but actor network theory is descriptive rather than foundational in explanatory terms ... it tells stories about 'how' relations assemble or don't" (2009, 141–142). He believes instead that ANT is better thought of as a "family of material-semiotic tools, sensibilities, and methods of analysis ... a toolkit for telling interesting stories about, and interfering in, ... relations. More profoundly, it is a sensibility to the messy practices of relationality and materiality of the world" (Law 2009, 141–142).

Acknowledging the disparate nature of the works in the ANT corpus, Latour draws out three traits that he believes can help identify whether a study should be considered part of the ANT diaspora or not (2005, 10–11). Unsurprisingly, these traits relate to the fundamental aspects of ANT we have already discussed. The first of these is that non-humans are not only part of the narrative in these studies, but they are also actors in them. While this aspect of ANT may seem counter-intuitive when encountered for the first time, it is a critical aspect of the theory and it will be discussed in detail below. The second test concerns the nature of the social in these studies: If the social is considered a stable, hidden force that shapes the different elements of a situation, rather than something consisting of those elements and their various relations to each other, then the study is not part of the ANT corpus but rather a work of the "sociology of the social". Finally, if a work focuses on deconstruction, rather than tracing new connection and associations between entities, then it is not part of the ANT diaspora.

The remainder of this section provides a detailed discussion of the core concepts of ANT that will be employed in the ethnography chapters that follow and examines how these concepts have been applied by others to understand digital media. This discussion draws upon a broad range of theorists and studies, the selection of which is guided by Latour's three traits discussed above, and by their utility for analysing the chapters that follow.

Actors. An early indication of what Callon and Latour mean by an "actor" appears in their foundational 1981 paper, where they draw upon the semiotics of Algirdas Greimas and state that actors are not limited to humans (1981, 301n8). The reference to semiotics is not meant to imply a focus on texts, but in fact extends to anything: "settings, machines, bodies, and programming languages as well as texts" (Akrich and Latour 1992, 259). The principles of this "material semiotics", as it is sometimes referred to, are drawn out in more detail by Law and

Mol: "Within material semiotics an entity counts as an actor if it makes a perceptible difference. Active entities are relationally linked with one another in webs. They make a difference to each other ... they enact each other" (Law and Mol 2008, 58). Agency is therefore understood in material semiotics not as a property of an individual actor, but rather as a property of the "webs of materialised relations": "An actor does not act alone. It acts in relation to other actors, lined up with them" (Law and Mol 2008, 58).

Understanding agency in this way goes some distance to addressing the prima facie counter-intuitive nature of ANT's claim that non-humans can be actors. Law and Mol (2008) confront this directly (and somewhat playfully) in their discussion of Cumbrian sheep during the outbreak of foot and mouth disease in the UK in 2001. They argue that when we ask if a sheep is an actor, the response we expect is framed by the notion of mastery: The sheep is either a master of its situation or it is simply being mastered by humans, the latter alternative being the only sensible response. They argue, however, that this division between mastery and being mastered when thinking about actors is rejected in ANT because of the distributed nature of agency, as discussed above, and because an actor "is not in control": "To act is not to master, for the results of what is being done are often unexpected ... In order to make a difference, a sheep does not need to be a strategist" (Law and Mol 2008, 58).

Latour also tries to resolve some of the misunderstandings concerning how ANT scholars use the term "actor": "The word actor has been open to ... misunderstanding ... 'Actor' in the Anglo-Saxon tradition is always a human intentional individual actor and is most often contrasted with mere 'behavior'" (1998, Section 3). He continues, in a vein similar to Law and Mol: "An 'actor' in ANT is a semiotic definition – an actant –, that is, something that acts or to which activity is granted by others. It implies no special motivation of human individual actors, nor of humans in general. An actant can literally be anything provided it is granted to be the source of an action" (Latour 1998, Section 3).[9] So not only are sheep treated as actors in ANT studies, but so are other creatures like insects (Akrich 1993) and scallops (Callon 1986), as well as a wide variety of other things such as Enterprise Resource Planning computer systems (McMaster and Wastell 2005), scientific papers, and signed cheques (Callon 1991, 140, 156).

Networks. The concept of "networks" has already been anticipated by the mention of "webs" in the foregoing discussion of material semiotics. Looking more closely at the usage of this latter term, Law states that ANT treats "everything in the social and natural worlds as a continuously generated effect of the webs of relations within which they are located ... its studies explore and characterize [these] webs ..." (2009, 141). While the term "assemblage" is sometimes also used (for example, Latour 2005, 7), "network" is the preferred term within the corpus, although, like the word "actor", Latour argues that what ANT scholars mean by the word has been misunderstood. He explains that the usage of the word in the 1980s, when ANT was conceived, was different to how it is used now. He argues that now it means "transport *without* deformation" (Latour 1999a, 15) and is "a term used for sewage, telephones and the Internet" (Latour in Gane 2004, 83). However, in the older usage it "clearly meant a series of transformations – translations, transductions – which could not be captured by any of the traditional terms of social theory" (Latour 1999a, 15). To get a clearer understanding of the core concept of networks, it is therefore important first to understand what ANT scholars mean by these terms.

The terms transform, translate, and transduce are used interchangeably by ANT scholars, although "translate" is the preferred term within the literature.[10] The idea of translation is at the heart of ANT, and Latour (2005, 106) in fact uses the term "the sociology of translation" as another name for ANT, and Callon also uses this term in his seminal 1986 paper as the name of his theoretical position (1986). What ANT scholars mean when they speak of translations derives from a crucial distinction they draw between "intermediaries" and "mediators". According to Latour, an intermediary "is what transports meaning or force without transformation: defining its inputs is enough to define its outputs" (2005, 39). Because of this lack of impact and its predictability, the complexity of an intermediary can be ignored, and even the intermediary itself can fade into the background or be forgotten. Latour gives the example of a properly functioning computer as an intermediary (2005, 39). Elaborating on his example, we could argue that while it is exceedingly complicated, its role in certain social situations (in an email exchange, for example) does not need to take account of this complexity, and in fact the computer itself can mostly likely also be neglected entirely within the accounts of those situations.

Unlike intermediaries, mediators "transform, translate, distort, and modify the meaning or the elements they are supposed to carry … their input is never a good predictor of their output; their specificity has to be taken into account every time" (Latour 2005, 39). For example, continuing with the computing theme, we will see in the ethnography chapters that computer software applications, far from being dutiful intermediaries, were often mediators in the ANT sense and attention to the specificity of these applications is an important part of the stories told in these chapters. For the "sociology of the social", the world is made of few mediators but many intermediaries, which are involved in transporting the effects of society, "social factors", while for ANT there are an "endless" number of mediators, some of which become intermediaries on rare occasions (Latour 2005, 40, 105).

Having now seen that mediators are the source of translations in ANT, the common meaning of "mediate", concerning bringing about agreement or reconciliation, gets us most of the way to understanding the ANT definition of "translation". Callon, drawing upon the work of philosopher Michel Serres, states that "translation involves creating convergences and homologies by relating things that were previously different ... [it is] the expression of a shared desire to arrive at the same result" (1980, 211). Similarly, Latour defines "translation" as "a relation that ... induces two mediators into coexisting" (2005, 108). Also, it is an important corollary of the fact that actors can be almost anything within ANT, as discussed above, that mediators related by the process of translations can be heterogeneous (Callon and Law 1989, 58–59, 77).

Paraphrasing Harman's (2009, 15) simple example of these concepts, when a general gives an order to capture a city that order is not simply communicated, as is, to all the soldiers involved. Rather, it involves a massive amount of mediation with higher echelon commanders drawing up detailed plans that are then passed to lower echelon commanders who translate them into orders for individual officers. These officers must then translate these orders into a language and style that will motivate the soldiers under their command into action and direct their activities. The individual soldiers must then translate these orders into their own physical activities on the battlefield.

These translations are not simply about faithfully rendering something from one "language" into another, from the language of the general into the language of the enlisted soldier, but more importantly, they are about translating interests: "Offering new interpretations of these interests and channelling people in different directions" (Latour 1987, 117). Continuing the example above, the general's interest in capturing a particular city may be interpreted by lower echelon commanders to require attacking airfields and railway yards in a different city because it is judged by those commanders to be integral to the target city's defence. Also, as Law (2003) has stressed, interests are not always translated with fidelity. For example, an individual officer may be concerned that soldiers under her command are panicked, and so interprets the order from her commander to move on an enemy position in such a way as to minimize the stress on her soldiers. While this attack approach might make them less damaging to the enemy, it gains the soldiers' cooperation by reducing their risk of taking casualties while simultaneously conforming to the letter of the order, thereby allowing the officer to avoid court-martial.

The different acts of translation between the mediators in these examples create associations between them, and it is at this point that what Latour describes as a more precise definition of the sociology of associations can be given: "There is no society, no social realm, and no social ties, *but there exist translations between mediators that may generate traceable associations*" (2005, 108). A network, or more precisely an actor-network, can therefore be defined as this web of associations created by mediators, which "are enacted, enabled, and adapted by their associates while in their turn enacting, enabling and adapting these [associates]" (Mol 2010, 260). That is, it represents "flows of translations" (Latour 2005, 132) created by the work of actors.

Callon (1986), in an early formulation of the concept of translation, defined it as a process that had four phases. Although later versions of ANT adopted the less rigid formulation discussed above, Callon's approach continues to be employed by some scholars (see, for example, Mähring et al. (2004) and Adamopoulos et al. (2014)). While his approach will not be adopted here in its entirety, his concept of problematization, and the emphasis he places on the conflicts that can arise when actors try to align other actors' interests with their own, provide insights into the translation process that will allow for a more nuanced approach to analysing some of the many different examples of translations encountered in the chapters that follow.

For Callon (1986, 203–211), problematization is the process whereby the problem the nascent actor-network will be employed to address is posed by the actors initiating the formation of that actor-network. During this process, the initiating actors also identify and define the other actors that they envisage being part of the actor-network, based on their interpretations of what these other actors are, what their interests might be, and the other associations they might have. Since these other actors can resist the definitions given to them by the problematization, or be involved in other problematizations that defined them in conflicting ways, the initiating actors can become involved in "trials of strength" (Callon 1986, 207) and multilateral negotiations with these other actors to create the desired alignment of interests. During these conflicts, the initiating actors can use various strategies to redefine the other actors and cut them off from competing problematizations. These other actors become enrolled in the actor-network if this process of aligning interests is successful: They take on the roles within the actor-network proposed for them in the problematization or the renegotiated version of these roles defined during the process.

Translations, therefore, regardless of their formulation within ANT, require work. Latour emphasizes the centrality of work to the understanding of how actor-networks are constructed: "What is important in the word network is the word *work*. You need work in order to make the connection" (Latour in Gane 2004, 83). He goes as far as to say that at one point he toyed with the term "work-net" instead to underscore the difference between the current common use of the word and the way it is used by ANT scholars because, as he cautions, "A network is not made of nylon thread, words or any durable substance but is the trace left behind by some moving agent ... it has to be traced anew by the passage of another vehicle, another circulating entity" (Latour 2005, 132).[11]

Sometimes networks can appear as actors themselves: "If a network acts as a single block, then it disappears, to be replaced by the action itself and the seemingly simple author of that action" (Law 1992, 385). Law illustrates this idea by saying that a single, simple actor like "a working television, a well-managed bank or a healthy body ... mask the networks that produce [them]" (1992, 385). ANT theorists refer to this "masking" effect as "punctualisation" or "blackboxing", and such networks can in turn be treated as single actors within other networks (Callon 1991, 153; Latour 1999b, 304; Law 1992, 385), although this situation is precarious for reasons that will be discussed below.

Examples of ANT studies. Law states that ANT is not an abstract approach, but one grounded in empirical case studies, and that it can only be understood in the context of those studies (2009, 141; see also 2003, 1, 8). With this in mind, having now provided theoretical outlines of the fundamental concepts of actors and networks, some archetypical ANT studies will be discussed below that will both explore these concepts further as well as introduce some additional ANT concepts that will be employed in the chapters that follow.

The first study is Madeline Akrich's account (1993) of the operation of a Swedish briquette-making machine in Nicaragua. Law describes it as "an exemplary actor-network study", and the description of it here paraphrases his English language version of it (2003, 2–4). The machine in question took by-products from the Swedish forest industry (for example sawdust, shavings, and offcuts) and turned them into briquettes to be burned as fuel in the processes of other industries. The Swedes wondered if Nicaragua, which was short of fuel, could use the machine to convert tropical forest waste. However, because the forests in Nicaragua were remote from populated areas and held by the Contras at the time, forest waste could not be used. Experiments were tried with other waste products. Waste products from the rice industry did not work, but cotton stalks, which were waste from the cotton industry, did form durable briquettes. These were also plentiful, and farmers were required by law to dispose of them to keep pests that might breed in the stalks under control. But the cotton stalks needed to be collected from the fields, and a machine from Sudan was used to collect and bale the stalks. It also turned out that while Swedish industry used the briquettes made from their forest industry's waste, Nicaraguan industry was not interested, as their boilers could not burn the briquettes. The briquettes however were suitable for different markets: domestic users and bakeries.

Drawing upon and elaborating Law's analysis of this case study (2003, 3), we can see a number of key ANT concepts in action. First, it is a story of two networks, one Swedish and one Nicaraguan. In the Swedish context, the network is one of Swedish sawmills, their wood waste products, a machine to convert the waste to briquettes, and industrial buyers, just to list some of the main actors. In the Nicaraguan context, the network consists of cotton farmers, laws, cotton stalks, the Swedish machine modified to handle cotton stalks, the machine's advocates, a Sudanese bailing machine, domestic buyers, and bakers. In both cases, heterogeneous networks of human and non-human actors are involved. These networks also transform and define their actors by the different ways they act upon each other: For example, cotton stalks are transformed from useless and potentially biologically harmful waste into useful raw material for the machine. The machine is also transformed through its operation in the Nicaraguan environment and redefined in that new network.

We can see therefore that the Nicaraguan network was formed through a series of translation processes that required work: For example, different raw materials were experimented with, farmers were approached, and buyers were sought out and contracted with. Some of these processes were successful, while others were unsuccessful, with the successful ones bringing in new actors into the network to help the network achieve its aims. ANT scholars typically refer to the successful inclusion of a new actor into a network as an "enrolment" (see for example Callon and Law 1982).

The second study is from Law's (1986) analysis of the Portuguese trading empire of the 15th and 16th Century, which is from one of the seminal works of ANT referred to earlier. In this study, Law describes how new types of ship rigging transform and enrol certain previously adverse and dangerous winds into new sources of propulsion for the Portuguese ships (1986, 240). However, one of the key features of enrolment is that it is precarious, and therefore so are networks, since their stability depends on their actors remaining enrolled within them: "Building and maintaining networks is an uphill battle ... enrolment is precarious ... links and nodes in the network do not last all by themselves but instead need constant maintenance work, the support of other links and nodes" (Law 2003, 3). This idea of constant maintenance work is prominent in the Portuguese study: The stability of that network, the trading empire, required the regular transit of ships from Lisbon to Goa or Calicut in India and back again so the centre could maintain the enrolment of the peripheries' actors within the network (Law 1986, 240–241, 2009, 146).

Sometimes, however, in spite of attempts to maintain the network's stability, actors can cease to perform the roles assigned to them by other actors, and the network comes apart. An example of this comes from Callon's (1986) study of marine biologists who attempted to develop a conservation strategy for scallops in St. Brieuc Bay in France, which is another of the seminal studies mentioned above. The biologists enrolled the scallops through laying collectors in the bay for the scallop larvae to attach and grow protected from predators. They also enrolled the local fishermen, negotiating with them to stay away from the collectors, convincing them that allowing the scallops to thrive in the collectors will lead to an increase over time in the bay's rapidly depleting scallop population. In the first year this network was stable, but in the second year it began to come apart: The next generation of larvae failed to attach to the collectors. The scallop larvae no longer perform the role within the network for which they were enrolled. Similarly, the fishermen one day some time later decided to harvest the collectors for the mature scallops that had grown from the initial larvae and destroyed the collectors in the process: The translation by the marine biologists of the fishermen's interest in short-term gain into an interest in long-term sustainable fishing grounds had therefore failed.

Having completed our general outline of ANT, we now explore some of the ways it has been applied to digital media. As with the discussion concerning the application of Assemblage Theory, the purpose here is to show that ANT has been successfully employed to analyse a wide range of situations and to highlight specific studies that provide useful insights for the situations encountered in the ethnography chapters. Rivera and Cox (2016) discuss the failed attempt by leaders of a project at a Mexican university to get the stakeholders of that project to form an online community around a collaborative technology platform. They analyse the failure in terms of the inability of the project leaders to translate the interests of the stakeholders into something compatible with that technology. Rivera and Cox state that the project leaders' decision to introduce this technology was guided by their interest in making the implementation of the project transparent to them without having to incur the cost of visiting the different campuses. The project leaders' attempts to enrol stakeholders into using this new platform failed however, and the reasons for this included the inability of the leaders and the platform to translate the interests of the stakeholders to ones consistent with its adoption because of, for example, its limited features, its instability, and the adequacy of pre-existing tools. Napoli (2014, 344) invokes ANT to describe computer algorithms as "the complex intermingling of human and nonhuman actors". Following Ullman (1997), he argues that although humans are indispensable to their coding and maintenance, "over time, and with the disparate inputs of an expanding number of individuals within specific, compartmentalized contexts, an algorithmic system becomes more difficult for any one person to understand in its entirety, and thus to some extent 'takes on a life of its own'" (Napoli 2014, 344). Adamopoulos et al. (2014) discuss how changes made over time to Internet-based financial investment services had worked to translate the interests of the investors that used them, highlighting the ability of non-human Internet technology actors to translate the interests of human actors. Furthermore, they found that these non-human actors are sometimes so powerful that they become the preeminent actors in the network.

ANT has also been used to analyse the adoption of social media platforms (Singh and Kurian 2014), as well as to examine how sociality (Van Dijck 2013) and controversies (Poell et al. 2014) manifest on them. It has been used to examine the impact of new media technologies on journalistic practices (Schmitz Weiss and Domingo 2010; Turner 2005), to evaluate the implementation of an ICT4D project (Díaz Andrade and Urquhart 2010), to frame avatars as mediators in virtual worlds such as *EverQuest* and *Second Life* (Jensen 2009), and to examine the translation processes engaged in by older people adopting Internet technologies (Lepa and Tatnall 2006).

Finally in this section we turn to ANT's critics, focusing primarily on criticisms relevant to the particular construction of it developed above, and address how these relate to the theory's application in the following chapters. Criticisms relating to the way ANT treats agency come in different forms, and one such attack focuses on the perceived ascription of agency to non-humans. Critics see this as problematic because, for example, it fetishizes non-humans (Hornborg 2017) and reiterates humans as the "standard measure of agency to which non-humans are elevated" (Khong 2003, 702–703). Sayes (2014, 143) argues that while some of Latour's more polemical statements may provide a basis for such criticisms, these criticisms are not sustainable when the actual ways non-humans are incorporated into ANT studies are examined. Similarly, Sismondo argues that in practice ANT studies "tend to downplay any agency that non-humans might have …" (2010, 90). Also, as we saw above, the account of ANT given here does not ascribe agency to non-humans directly, but rather takes agency to be a property of the actor-network, rather than of the individual actors that comprise it.[12]

Another form these criticisms of ANT's treatment of agency comes in is to accuse it of denying the importance of human intention to accounts of agency: "Humans have, and most non-humans do not have, intentionality, which is necessary for action on traditional accounts of agency", therefore, "to treat humans and non-humans symmetrically, ANT has to deny that intentionality is necessary for action" (Sismondo 2010, 90). We have seen, however, that in practice, the intentions of humans feature prominently in ANT's accounts, be they French marine biologists, Portuguese sail makers, or Nicaraguan machinists. The resolution of this contradiction comes down to critics resting too heavily on polemical overstatements concerning the similarities between humans and non-humans in ANT and to a misunderstanding of how human intention is expressed in the version of ANT outlined above: Specifically, it is not so much that humans do not have intentions, but rather that those intentions are mediated through a web of other humans and non-humans who both act upon and also enact those intentions. Because of this, the actors acting upon the actor with the intention in question influence the formulation of that intention, while those that enact it can do so in unintended or unexpected ways, sometimes frustrating it, causing the intention to be modified or abandoned. This complex interrelationship between intent, agency, humans, and non-human actors will be explored in detail within the ethnography chapters.

ANT is also criticized for not engaging in political critique, although the specific charge is framed in different ways. For example, Winner (1993, 370) accuses ANT scholars engaged in technology studies of not expressing sufficient interest in how the development of technologies favours elite interests over those of others. Whether this is true in general of ANT technology studies does not concern us here, as the ethnography chapters of this book highlight with disconcerting frequency how video producers' online distribution practices are shaped by elite interests that they have very little power to influence.

Another framing of the charge that ANT lacks political critique is based on a more general criticism of ethnography, which forms the methodological basis of ANT studies. Kipnis (2015, 53–54) summarizes this criticism by saying that it is difficult if not impossible to gain the kind of access to centres of power that would be required to conduct a critical ethnography of them. For example, observation of, and participation in, sensitive processes would typically not be allowed, and finding informants within such centres willing to provide reliable testimony for a critical study would be difficult. Again, whether this is a problem for ANT (or ethnography) in general is not of concern here, as the ethnography chapters here do not attempt to study these centres of power directly, but rather map and critically assess the power relations my informants are in with such centres.

The final criticism of ANT addressed here claims that it merely provides a descriptive language rather than an explanatory framework (see for example, Michael 2016, 26). The ANT response to this criticism is not to deny it (in fact, as we saw above, Law embraces this aspect of ANT), but rather to call into question its framing. For example, Latour, after a long critique of the very idea of explanations within social sciences states that "the belief in the existence of a framework inside which events are inserted in order to be explained is the hallmark of non-reflexive social sciences. ... We have to write stories that do not start with a framework but that end up with [the] local and provisional ... Every time we deal with a new topic ... the explanation should be wholly different. Instead of explaining everything with the same cause and framework, ... we shall provide a one-off explanation, using a tailor-made cause" (1988b, 174). This is therefore not a rejection of explanation so much as a rejection of using pre-existing theoretical frameworks to arrive at them in favour of explanations emerging out of the specific sociological situation under investigation.

Staying with the detail of these situations is critical to such explanations according to Latour: "The achievement of such stories is a new relationship between historical detail and the grand picture. Since the latter is produced by the former, the reader will always want more details, not less, and will never wish to leave details in favour of getting at the general trend" (1988b, 174). As we saw in the introductory chapter, ethnography is a methodology that produces rich and detailed accounts of situations, and it is therefore unsurprising that it is an approach that is closely associated with ANT. Within these descriptions, ANT scholars painstakingly trace the dynamic web of processes that entangle actors with each other. This detail is required because these networks are not stable and physical things "out there … like a telephone, a freeway, or a sewage 'network'" (Latour 2005, 129), but rather must be assembled out of the myriad of elements that comprise an ethnographic investigation to understand how they are formed, what keeps them stable, and why they change or fail. Relating this perspective on explanation to the approach of this book, rather than adopting a pre-exiting framework to analyse online video such as participatory culture or political economy, the ethnography chapters trace in detail the different networks of which the producers and their videos were a part. In doing so, they explain the often-problematic situations encountered by these producers in terms of the specificity of those situations.

Assemblage Theory and ANT

The final section of this chapter examines the similarities and differences between Assemblage Theory and ANT. The scope of the discussion is limited to the specific concepts discussed in this chapter and to the particular interpretations and forms in which they have been represented here. The discussion will also be primarily focused on similarities and differences that have implications for the application of the theories to the chapters that follow, rather than be an abstract, metaphysical comparison.

Various scholars attest to the close relationship between the two theories. For example, John Law points out that "there is little difference between Deleuze's *agencement* … and the term 'actor network'" (2009, 146), which is a view echoed by Acuto and Curtis (2014, 5), who see the difference between the two terms as one of emphasis only. Law goes on to state that this similarity is indicated by the fact that both terms "refer to the provisional assembly of productive, heterogeneous, and … quite limited forms of ordering located in no larger overall order" (2009, 146). Harman stresses other aspects of their similarity: "DeLanda's assemblage theory and Latour's actor-network theory both refer to large syndicates of objects that interact even while remaining separable from the assemblies in which they participate. Both are anti-Copernicans who deny any poignant gap between humans and the world, and both also try to avoid the pseudo-revolution that denies such a gap only by turning humans and the world into equal partners" (2007, 3).[13] He also goes on to say elsewhere that both theories "emphasize change over stability, becoming over stasis, relation over substance" (Harman 2014, 124). A number of works also draw upon the conceptual vocabularies of both theories for their own purposes, treating them as compatible, and using their different terms either interchangeably or as a complement to each other (see, for example, Salovaara (2015), Rizzo (2015), Reid (2011), and Bennett (2005)).

Some contend, however, that the theories diverge in some respects. For example, in spite of his statements above, Harman also argues that the concepts of assemblages and actor-networks are not identical, but in fact have an important difference. His argument rests on a metaphysical consideration concerning the nature of time in both theories: He argues that Deleuze draws upon a Bergsonian notion of time, which is continuous, while Latour, on the contrary, draws upon Whitehead's discontinuous conception of time. Harman says the consequence of this is that Deleuzian assemblages are involved in continuous processes of becoming, while Latour's "last for only an instant, perishing in favour of a close successor that is not, strictly speaking, the *same* assemblage" (2014, 124–125; see also Harman 2009, 30–31). Even if we accept Harman's argument, actor-networks do not appear to be treated in the way he describes in practical applications of ANT. Reviewing the different case studies discussed in this chapter, actor-networks – be they empires, conservation projects, or initiatives turning waste into fuel – do not wink out of existence in an instant to be replaced by another in any practical sense, but rather appear to change over time in a continuous way, much like the way he argues Deleuzian assemblages do. Since our interest is with practical applications, Harman's metaphysical considerations can be set aside here.

Müller and Schurr, while pointing out that the "similarities between assemblage thinking and ANT are striking", also highlight differences that they believe complement each other, where one theory brings a perspective, emphasis or set of tools to bear that is not as well developed in the other (2016, 217). While the details of their argument are not directly relevant here because of the particular formulations of the two theories they use, their stance of treating these two theories as complementary (rather than as identical or incompatible) is the one adopted here. While the details of this complementarity will be addressed during the practical application of the theories, some general, theoretical remarks concerning it conclude this chapter.

Conclusion

As stated in the introduction to this chapter, the wider range of theoretical concepts, perspectives, and examples of practical applications offered by using both theories, rather than just one, allowed for more faithful and nuanced accounts of the rich and multifaceted situations encountered during the fieldwork. Redundancies and inconsistencies in these accounts due to using two different theoretical approaches are avoided because the theories (in the forms they have been presented in this chapter at least), although very similar, are not identical, while their differences offer complementary rather than conflicting insights.

One such complementary aspect concerns the processes that form, stabilize, and destabilize assemblages/actor-networks. On the one hand, the concepts of interests, translation, and enrolment from ANT provide useful categories within which to analyse the different aspects and stages of these processes, and they also help define the relationships between the different actors involved in them. Territorialization and deterritorialization, on the other hand, focus our attention on the spatial and homogenizing aspects of these stabilization/destabilization processes, while coding draws attention to their linguistic aspects. Also, through the concepts of diagrams and reterritorialization and the distinction drawn between relative and absolute deterritorialization, Assemblage Theory adds a virtual space in which to think about these stabilization/destabilization processes that complements ANT's predominant focus on actuality. Another complementary aspect concerns the features the theories ascribe to the elements that make up assemblages/actor-networks. While Assemblage Theory talks about a component's capacities, and whether the component is material or expressive, ANT draws our attention to whether actors are mediators or intermediaries. Also, while Assemblage Theory concerns itself with the properties of assemblages emerging from the processes acting upon these components, ANT focuses on tracing the associations that are created by those processes (which form actor-networks). Finally, ANT brings with it a wealth of applications produced by a multitude of scholars since the 1980s, which have helped develop its different concepts into robust and flexible empirical tools. On the other hand, this has meant that ANT has not developed in a theoretically cohesive way, unlike DeLanda's Assemblage Theory, which can therefore act as a theoretical touchstone as required.

The next three chapters apply the concepts developed here to close readings of the ethnographies of the subject producer groups, beginning with the video activist group visionOntv: These chapters frame the often complex arrangements of machines, humans, and other components that were part of the producers' video distribution practices as assemblages and actor-networks, identifying and analysing the different processes of formation, stabilization, and destabilization that their components underwent using the conceptual tools of these two theories. Since the chapters will be drawing upon both theories, to avoid confusion and for convenience's sake, references to the producers' particular arrangements will use the term assemblages throughout, even when the discussion concerns concepts specific to ANT, thereby avoiding the need to continually alternate between the terms assemblages and actor-networks in the chapters when referring to the same arrangement.

Notes

1 DeLanda uses the adjectives "emergent" and "synthetic" to refer to these properties of assemblages, although the former will only be used here for simplicity's sake and because it is assumed to be a term with which more readers are familiar.

2 Deleuze emphasizes the relationship between these two processes when he says, "there is no deterritorialization without an effort for reterritorialization" (Boutang and Pamart 1995, 13 cited in Fortier 2000; see also Deleuze and Guattari 1987, 508).

3 DeLanda's introduction of coding as a dimension is a break with Deleuze and Guattari. DeLanda does this to avoid introducing "strata" as an entity in addition to assemblages. See DeLanda (2006b, 123n21) for a discussion of this.

4 The term "coding" here being used of course in the manner above, and not in the sense of writing a computer application.

5 An assemblage with these parameter settings corresponds to Deleuze and Guattari's concept of "strata" according to DeLanda (2016, 26).

6 Deleuze and Guattari use the terms "molar" and "molecular" rather than "macro" and "micro" to describe these part-to-whole relationships. DeLanda argues that the Deleuzian terms do not directly correspond to his terms, although there is considerable overlap. See DeLanda (2006a, 252, 2006b, 126n7, 2016, 20–21, 127–128) for a discussion of how these different sets of concepts relate. It should be pointed out at this point, however, that tracing the Deleuzian terms to their origins in thermodynamics does sheds some additional light on the nature of assemblages. If we take a gas for example, it is composed of molecules. One property these molecules have is kinetic energy (which is a product of their mass and velocity), but they do not have individual temperatures. Temperature is a molar property, that is to say, it is the property of a large number of molecules taken together: Specifically, it is related to the statistical average of the kinetic energy of all the molecules in the gas. In the language of assemblages, it is also called an emergent property, as we have seen. See DeLanda (2010, 129) and Deleuze and Guattari (1987, 334–335) for additional discussions of this.

7 It should be noted, as Buchannan (2015, 383) points out, that *agencement* is Deleuze and Guattari's rendering of the German word *Komplex* (as in "Oedipal complex").

8 This review does not discuss the Deleuzian terms that appear in this literature that DeLanda does not employ in his schema, as they would require additional theoretical explanation that would not be used elsewhere in this book. Instead, the following review interprets such concepts within the DeLandian framework and presents them as such.

9 Latour's use of the term "actant" derives from Greimas (Blok and Jensen 2011, 17, 48). ANT scholars use both "actor" and "actant" in their studies, and many use them interchangeably, although Akrich and Latour (1992, 259) do draw a minor distinction, but one that is not significant here. In the ethnography chapters that follow, the term "actant" rather than "actor" will sometimes be used when referring to non-human entities because it is less jarring to the reader not accustomed to this theoretical approach. But this is for cosmetic purposes only, and conceptually the terms should be considered interchangeable throughout.

10 Similar to the use of the words actor and actant, "transform" will read more naturally than "translate" in some cases when analysing the ethnography chapters, where it will be used instead, although all three terms should be considered to be interchangeable throughout this book.

11 There is a subtly in Latour's use of the words trace and traceable that relate to his definition of networks that will not be explored here since it does not impact the analysis done in the following chapters. It concerns the nature of the sociological text, and can be found in Latour (2005, 127–133).

12 While this disposes of the criticism above, computer applications, which are the particular kind of non-humans that primarily feature in the ethnography chapters of this book, are not the kind that tend to attract the ire of critics in any case. For example, Hornborg states, "the purposes which define biotic entities presuppose a certain capacity for sentience and communication ... Amoebas, trees and humans are all equipped to register specific aspects of their environments and to somehow respond to them. ... Abiotic entities such as rocks or artifacts do not have such capacities" (2017, 98). Computer applications, however, purposefully register and respond to their environment, and therefore avoid this criticism.

13 To be "Anti-Copernican" for Harman means to be against the Kantian primacy of the human subject with respect to non-humans (Harman 2011, 45).

References

Acuto, Michele, and Simon Curtis. 2014. "Assemblage Thinking and International Relations." In *Reassembling International Theory: Assemblage Thinking and International Relations*, edited by M. Acuto, 1–15. London: Palgrave Pivot.

Adamopoulos, Arthur, Martin Dick, and Bill Davey. 2014. "Web Tools as Actors: The Case of Online Investing." In *Technological Advancements and the Impact of Actor-Network Theory*, edited by Tatnall Arthur, 252–259. Hershey, PA: IGI Global.

Akrich, M. 1993. *Inscription et Coordination Socio-Techniques: Anthropologie de Quelques Dispositifs Énergétiques*, École Nationale Supérieure des Mines de Paris, Paris.

Akrich, M., and B. Latour. 1992. "A Summary of a Convenient Vocabulary for the Semiotics of Human and Nonhuman Assemblies." In *Shaping Technology/Building Society: Studies in Sociotechnical Change*, edited by Wiebe Bijker and John Law, 259–264. Cambridge, MA: MIT Press.

Bennett, J. 2005. "The Agency of Assemblages and the North American Blackout." *Public Culture* no. 17 (3):445–466.

Bennett, J. 2009. *Vibrant Matter: A Political Ecology of Things*. Durham, NC: Duke University Press.

Blok, A., and T.E. Jensen. 2011. *Bruno Latour: Hybrid Thoughts in a Hybrid World*. London: Routledge.

Boutang, P.A., and M. Pamart. 1995. *L'abécédaire de Gilles Deleuze/ entretien, Claire Parnet*. Paris: Editions Montparnasse/Sodaperaga.

Buchanan, Ian. 2015. "Assemblage Theory and Its Discontents." *Deleuze Studies* no. 9 (3):382–392.

Bueger, Christian. 2014. "Thinking Assemblages Methodologically: Some Rules of Thumb." In *Reassembling International Theory: Assemblage Thinking and International Relations*, edited by M. Acuto, 58–66. London: Palgrave Pivot.

Callon, Michel. 1980. "Struggles and Negotiations to Define What is Problematic and What is Not: The Socio-Logic of Translation." *The Social Process of Scientific Investigation* no. 4:197–219.

Callon, Michel. 1986. "Some Elements of a Sociology of Translation: The Domestication of the Scallops and St Brieuac Fishermen." In *Power, Action and Belief*, edited by J. Law, 196–232. London: Routledge and Kegan Paul.

Callon, Michel. 1991. "Techno-Economic Networks and Irreversibility." In *A Sociology of Monsters: Essays on Power, Technology and Domination*, edited by J.Law, 132–161. London: Routledge.

Callon, Michel, and Bruno Latour. 1981. "Unscrewing the Big Leviathan: How Actors Macro-Structure Reality and How Sociologists Help Them to Do so." In *Advances in Social Theory and Methodology: Toward an Integration of Micro-and Macro-Sociologies*, edited by K. Knorr-Cetina and A.V. Cicourel, 277–303. Abingdon: Routledge.

Callon, Michel, and John Law. 1982. "On Interests and Their Transformation: Enrolment and Counter-Enrolment." *Social Studies of Science* no. 12 (4): 615–625.

Callon, Michel, and John Law. 1989. "On the Construction of Sociotechnical Networks: Content and Context Revisited." *Knowledge and Society* no. 8 (1):57–83.

Cremin, Colin. 2016. "Molecular Mario: The Becoming-Animal of Video Game Compositions." *Games and Culture* no. 11 (4):441–458.

De Paoli, S., and A. Kerr. 2009. The Cheating Assemblage in MMORPGs: Toward a Sociotechnical Description of Cheating. Paper read at *Breaking New Ground: Innovation in Games, Play, Practice and Theory. Proceedings of DiGRA 2009*, London, UK.

DeLanda, Manuel. 2005. *Intensive Science and Virtual Philosophy*. London: Continuum.

DeLanda, Manuel. 2006a. "Deleuzian Social Ontology and Assemblage Theory." In *Deleuze and the social*, edited by M. Fuglsang and B.M. Sørensen, 250–266. Edinburgh: Edinburgh University Press.

DeLanda, Manuel. 2006b. *A New Philosophy of Society: Assemblage Theory and Social Complexity*. London: Continuum (Kindle Edition).

DeLanda, Manuel. 2010. *Deleuze: History and Science*. New York: Atropos.

DeLanda, Manuel. 2011. *Philosophy and Simulation: The Emergence of Synthetic Reason*. London: Continuum (Kindle Edition).

DeLanda, Manuel. 2016. *Assemblage Theory*. Edinburgh: Edinburgh University Press.

Deleuze, G., and F. Guattari. 1987. *A Thousand Plateaus: Capitalism and Schizophrenia*. Minneapolis: University Of Minnesota Press.

Deleuze, Gilles, and Claire Parnet. 2006. *Dialogues II*. London: Continuum.

Díaz Andrade, Antonio, and Cathy Urquhart. 2010. "The Affordances of Actor Network Theory in ICT for Development Research." *Information Technology & People* no. 23 (4):352–374.

Fortier, A.M. 2000. *Migrant Belongings: Memory, Space, Identity*. Oxford: Berg.

Frosh, Paul, and Amit Pinchevski. 2014. "Media Witnessing and the Ripeness of Time." *Cultural Studies* no. 28 (4):594–610.

Gane, Nicholas. 2004. *The Future of Social Theory*. London: Continuum.

Harman, Graham. 2007. *Networks and Assemblages: The Rebirth of Things in Latour and DeLanda*. Goldsmiths College, University of London.

Harman, Graham. 2009. *Prince of Networks: Bruno Latour and Metaphysics*. Melbourne: Re-press.

Harman, Graham. 2011. *The Quadruple Object*. Alresford: Zero Books.

Harman, Graham. 2014. "Conclusions: Assemblage Theory and Its Future." In *Reassembling International Theory: Assemblage Thinking and International Relations*, edited by M. Acuto, 118–130. London: Palgrave Pivot.

Hess, Aaron. 2015. "The Selfie Assemblage." *International Journal of Communication* no. 9:1629–1646.

Hornborg, Alf. 2017. "Artifacts Have Consequences, Not Agency: Toward a Critical Theory of Global Environmental History." *European Journal of Social Theory* no. 20 (1):95–110.

Jensen, S.S. 2009. "Actors and Their Use of Avatars as Personal Mediators: An Empirical Study of Avatar-Based Sense-Makings and Communication Practices in the Virtual Worlds of *EverQuest* and *Second Life*." *MedieKultur. Journal of Media and Communication Research* no. 25 (47):29–44.

Khong, Lynnette. 2003. "Actants and Enframing: Heidegger and Latour on Technology." *Studies in History and Philosophy of Science Part A* no. 34 (4):693–704.

Kipnis, Andrew. 2015. "Agency between Humanism and Posthumanism: Latour and His Opponents." *HAU: Journal of Ethnographic Theory* no. 5 (2):43–58.

Langlois, Ganaele. 2013. "Participatory Culture and the New Governance of Communication: The Paradox of Participatory Media." *Television & New Media* no. 14 (2):91–105.

Latour, Bruno. 1987. *Science in Action: How to Follow Scientists and Engineers through Society*. Cambridge, MA: Harvard University Press.

Latour, Bruno. 1988a. *The Pasteurization of France*. Cambridge, MA: Harvard University Press.

Latour, Bruno. 1988b. "The Politics of Explanation: An Alternative." In *Knowledge and Reflexivity, New Frontiers in the Sociology of Knowledge*, edited by Steve Woolgar, 155–176. London: Sage.

Latour, Bruno. 1998. *On Actor-Network Theory: A Few Clarifications*. nettime mailing lists: mailing lists for networked cultures, politics, and tactics, [cited October 15 2012]. Available from www.nettime.org/Lists-Archives/nettime-l-9801/msg00019.html.

Latour, Bruno. 1999a. "On Recalling ANT." In *Actor Network Theory and After*, edited by J. Law and J. Hassard, 93–95. Oxford: Blackwell.

Latour, Bruno. 1999b. *Pandora's Hope: Essays on the Reality of Science Studies*. Cambridge, MA: Harvard University Press.

Latour, Bruno. 2005. *Reassembling the Social*. Oxford: Oxford University Press.

Law, John. 1986. "On the Methods of Long-Distance Control: Vessels, Navigation and the Portuguese Route to India." In *Power, Action and Belief: A New Sociology of Knowledge?*, edited by John Law, 234–263. London: Routledge & Kegan Paul.

Law, John. 1992. "Notes on the Theory of the Actor-Network: Ordering, Strategy, and Heterogeneity." *Systemic Practice and Action Research* no. 5 (4):379–393.

Law, John. 2003. Traduction/Trahison: Notes on ANT. www.lancaster.ac.uk/sociology/research/publications/papers/law-traduction-trahison.pdf.

Law, John. 2004. *After Method: Mess in Social Science Research*. London: Routledge.

Law, John. 2009. "Actor Network Theory and Material Semiotics." In *The New Blackwell Companion to Social Theory*, edited by B. Turner, 141–158. Oxford: Wiley-Blackwell.

Law, John, and Annemarie Mol. 2008. "The Actor-Enacted: Cumbrian Sheep in 2001." In *Material Agency: Towards a Non-anthropocentric Approach*, edited by Carl Knappett and Lambros Malafouris, 57–77. New York: Springer.

Lenzner, Ben. 2014. "The Emergence of Occupy Wall Street and Digital Video Practices: Tim Pool, Live Streaming and Experimentations in Citizen Journalism." *Studies in Documentary Film* no. 8 (3):251–266.

Lepa, Jerzy, and Arthur Tatnall. 2006. "Using Actor-Network Theory to Understanding Virtual Community Networks of Older People Using the Internet." *Journal of Business Systems, Governance and Ethics* no. 1 (4):1–14.

Mähring, Magnus, Jonny Holmström, Mark Keil, and Ramiro Montealegre. 2004. "Trojan Actor-Networks and Swift Translation: Bringing Actor-Network Theory to IT Project Escalation Studies." *Information Technology & People* no. 17 (2):210–238.

McMaster, Tom, and David Wastell. 2005. "The Agency of Hybrids: Overcoming the Symmetrophobic Block." *Scandinavian Journal of Information Systems* no. 17 (1):175–182.

Michael, Mike. 2016. *Actor-Network Theory: Trials, Trails and Translations.* London: Sage.

Mol, Annemarie. 2010. "Actor-Network Theory: Sensitive Terms and Enduring Tensions." *Kölner Zeitschrift für Soziologie und Sozialpsychologie. Sonderheft* no. 50:253–269.

Müller, Martin, and Carolin Schurr. 2016. "Assemblage Thinking and Actor-Network Theory: Conjunctions, Disjunctions, Cross-Fertilisations." *Transactions of the Institute of British Geographers* no. 41 (3):217–229. doi:10.1111/tran.12117.

Napoli, Philip M. 2014. "Automated Media: An Institutional Theory Perspective on Algorithmic Media Production and Consumption." *Communication Theory* no. 24 (3):340–360.

Patton, Paul. 2010. *Deleuzian Concepts: Philosophy, Colonization, Politics.* Stanford, CA: Stanford University Press.

Phillips, John. 2006. "Agencement/Assemblage." *Theory, Culture & Society* no. 23 (2–3):108–109. doi:10.1177/026327640602300219.

Poell, Thomas, Jeroen De Kloet, and Guohua Zeng. 2014. "Will the Real Weibo Please Stand Up? Chinese Online Contention and Actor-Network Theory." *Chinese Journal of Communication* no. 7 (1):1–18.

Reid, Alexander. 2010. Exposing Assemblages: Unlikely Communities of Digital Scholarship, Video, and Social Networks. *Enculturation* 8. http://enculturation.net/exposing-assemblages.

Reid, Alexander. 2011. "Social Media Assemblages in Digital Humanities: From Backchannel to Buzz." In *Teaching Arts and Science with the New Social Media (Cutting-edge Technologies in Higher Education, Volume 3)*, edited by Charles Wankel, 321–338. Bingley, UK: Emerald Group Publishing Limited.

Rivera, Gibran, and Andrew M. Cox. 2016. "An Actor-Network Theory Perspective to Study the Non-adoption of a Collaborative Technology Intended to Support Online Community Participation." *Academia Revista Latinoamericana de Administración* no. 29 (3):347–365.

Rizzo, Teresa. 2015. "FCJ-177 Television Assemblages." *The Fibreculture Journal* (24):106–126.

Salovaara, Inka. 2015. "Media Spaces of Fluid Politics Participatory Assemblages and Networked Narratives." *Media Transformations* no. 11:10–29.

Sampson, T. 2007. "The Accidental Topology of Digital Culture: How the Network Becomes Viral." *Transformations* (14):1–13.

Savat, D. 2010. "(Dis) Connected: Deleuze's Superject and the Internet." In *International Handbook of Internet Research*, edited by Jeremy Hunsinger, Lisbeth Klastrup and Matthew Allen, 423–436. London: Springer.

Sayes, Edwin. 2014. "Actor–Network Theory and Methodology: Just What Does It Mean to Say That Nonhumans Have Agency?" *Social Studies of Science* no. 44 (1):134–149.

Schmitz Weiss, Amy, and David Domingo. 2010. "Innovation Processes in Online Newsrooms as Actor-Networks and Communities of Practice." *New Media & Society* no. 12 (7):1156–1171.

Singh, Mohini, and Jayan Kurian. 2014. "Evolving Digital Communication: An Actor-Network Analysis of Social Networking Sites." In *Technological Advancements and the Impact of Actor-Network Theory*, edited by Arthur Tatnall, 222–237. Hershey, PA: IGI Global.

Sismondo, S. 2010. *An Introduction to Science and Technology Studies*. 2nd ed. Malden, MA: Wiley-Blackwell.

Tan, L. 2013. "Museums and Cultural Memory in an Age of Networks." *International Journal of Cultural Studies* no. 16 (4):383–399.

Taylor, T.L. 2009. "The Assemblage of Play." *Games and Culture* no. 4 (4):331–339.

Thorburn, Elise Danielle. 2014. "Social Media, Subjectivity, and Surveillance: Moving on from Occupy, the Rise of Live Streaming Video." *Communication and Critical/Cultural Studies* no. 11 (1):52–63.

Turner, Fred. 2005. "Actor-Networking the News." *Social Epistemology* no. 19 (4):321–324.

Ullman, Ellen. 1997. *Close to the Machine: Technophilia and Its Discontents*. San Francisco, CA: City Lights Books.

Van Dijck, Jose. 2013. "Facebook and the Engineering of Connectivity: A Multi-layered Approach to Social Media Platforms." *Convergence* no. 19 (2):141–155.

Winner, Langdon. 1993. "Upon Opening the Black Box and Finding It Empty: Social Constructivism and the Philosophy of Technology." *Science, Technology, & Human Values* no. 18 (3):362–378.

Wise, J.M. 2005. "Assemblage." In *Gilles Deleuze: Key Concepts*, edited by Charles Stivale, 77–87. Montreal: McGill-Queen's University Press.

Wise, J.M. 2012. "Attention and assemblage in the clickable world." In *Communication Matters: Materialist approaches to media, mobility, and networks*, edited by J Packer and Stephen B. Crofts Wiley, 159–172. Abingdon: Routledge.

4 VisionOntv
Video Activists

This chapter examines visionOntv's video distribution practices, analysing the processes that the human, machine, and other constituent components of these practices were subject to, within an Assemblage Theory and ANT framework, as visionOntv pursued its goal of fostering communities of social change on the Internet through the use of activist video.[1] The various activities visionOntv undertook in pursuit of this goal, as mentioned in Chapter 2, included the production and distribution of videos, the training of others to produce and distribute videos, and the development of a platform for the purpose of distributing these and other activist videos, as well as for the purpose of being a model platform for other video activist groups to adopt.

The first section of this chapter examines how visionOntv went about making and distributing videos, highlighting the precarious nature of the assemblage they created for these activities and analysing both the stabilization processes they undertook to maintain it and the destabilization processes to which it was subjected. The second section addresses the different "translation" (Callon 1980, 211; Latour 2005, 108) and "territorialization" (DeLanda 2006b, 12) processes visionOntv employed to not only enrol audiences for those videos within their assemblage, but also to facilitate discussions about them, which they saw as central to their goal of fostering communities of social change. The third section explores how visionOntv enrolled and maintained volunteers within their assemblage, who were crucial to its operation, focusing on issues related to the translation of the volunteers' interests. The fourth section looks at visionOntv's plans, and the challenges they faced in implementing these, to use their platform as the basis of a "macro assemblage" that would encompass their own "micro assemblage" (DeLanda 2006a, 252) and the micro assemblages of other video activist groups who adopted their distribution platform. We will see from the analysis in these sections that visionOntv faced considerable resistance from the different technologies and people they tried to enrol to create their video distribution assemblage, and even when they did succeed in enrolling them, substantial ongoing effort was required to maintain them as part of what proved to be a precarious and contested assemblage that ultimately fell short of what visionOntv required.

These first four sections analyse visionOntv's situation during the 2011/12 period of fieldwork. The final section revisits the findings from the earlier sections in the light of the 2016/17 fieldwork. In particular, it frames and analyses the change of identity visionOntv was undergoing during 2016/17 in response to continuing difficulties from the earlier period within the concept of "diagrams" (DeLanda 2006b, 30, 2011, Appendix).

The Precariousness of Video Distribution

VisionOntv's online video platform was the central element of their venture and the primary place they directed people to view their videos. It was a large and complex website built on the Liferay content management system that aggregated thousands of videos. The main features of the website were the various video "channels" it contained, which organized their videos, and those they curated, under different themes. For example, one of the main channels was called "Grassroots", and it aggregated videos concerning various left-wing grassroots activities in the UK relating to activism, campaigning, and direct action. The different channel pages had Miro Community embedded within them, which was a free, open source video aggregation software platform developed and distributed by the Participatory Culture Foundation.

The videos themselves were not hosted by visionOntv, but rather on third-party video hosting platforms like YouTube and Blip, and then linked to Miro Community in three main ways. One method involved directly linking individual videos from the hosting services. This could be done by anyone with administrator access to the visionOntv platform, which included visionOntv's two founding members plus a few other trusted volunteers and associates. The videos were selected on the basis of what the administrator thought would constitute a worthwhile addition to a specific channel. The other two methods involved the linking of an RSS feed from specific accounts of third parties on different video hosting services into one of the channels. One of these methods involved a "trusted feed", where all the videos upload to a specific YouTube, Blip, or other video account by a person or organization trusted by a visionOntv platform administrator would automatically be linked through to the relevant channel on an ongoing basis. The other method functioned in a similar way, except that the person or organization was not sufficiently trusted, and so Miro Community queued their videos up for individual approval or rejection by an administrator.

The processes for enrolling some of these distribution technologies into visionOntv's assemblage required considerable work and were sometimes fraught with difficulty and failure. As we saw in Chapter 3, this situation is typical of actor-networks: Work is needed to make the connections of which they are composed and is therefore a fundamental aspect of them (Latour in Gane 2004, 83), but the making of these connections is an "uphill battle" and precarious (Law 2003, 3). One example of this concerned visionOntv's attempt, at the outset of their venture, to use peer-to-peer torrent file technologies for their platform, which would have allowed users to download, rather than merely stream, visionOntv's videos. They were interested in this technology because they had originally imagined visionOntv as a screening network, where activists would download videos and screen them in venues in their local area, such as in pubs, homes, and community centres. These screenings were seen as ways of achieving visionOntv's mission of fostering communities of social change via the Internet and built upon visionOntv co-founder Hamish's experience at Undercurrents, where he would conduct similar screenings, bringing videos on physical media, such as VHS tapes, to the venues. VisionOntv believed that geographically dispersed users watching videos alone was an "isolated, individualistic, and disempowering" experience and an inferior way of building activist communities. They were, however, unable to make the torrent technology work the way they wanted it to work, and therefore abandoned their attempts to enrol it within the visionOntv assemblage. This situation can be understood as a failed translation: An unsuccessful attempt by visionOntv's founders at "relating things that were previously different" (Callon 1980, 211), in this case visionOntv's founders' requirements and their other technologies, on the one hand, and the torrent technology, on the other.

This failed translation saw them turn to video hosting platforms instead. VisionOntv did not believe, however, that the kinds of venues activists were likely to be able to access for screenings would have reliable enough Wi-Fi to provide uninterrupted and reasonable quality video from these platforms, so the idea of the screening network was abandoned in favour of focusing on an online-only audience. The enrolment processes for video hosting platforms were not without their own problems however. One example of this concerned the difficulties visionOntv had adapting RSS technology to their needs. They had made five different attempts, using five different volunteer programmers, to use RSS technology to syndicate videos from accounts on YouTube and other hosting platforms to the Miro Community software and the Liferay system, and while the final attempt had solved most of the issues related to the feeds, some problems still remained. As we shall see in the third section concerning volunteers, the reason that visionOntv had difficulty transforming these different technologies so that they could coexist went beyond simply technical incompatibility, but also included their inability to translate the interests of the volunteer programmers.

Even when they are completed successfully, enrolments are precarious, with work required to maintain them (Law 2003, 3), and so it was with the video hosting platforms, which became involved in different processes that threatened to destabilize their enrolment within visionOntv's assemblage. One such example concerns a problem that developed with one of the feeds from Blip causing celebrity and general entertainment videos to appear on one of visionOntv's channels. Upon investigation, visionOntv believed changes made to the Blip hosting platform were the cause of the problem. This situation threatened to destabilize the identity of visionOntv's assemblage: As DeLanda (2006b, 28) states, "the identity of any assemblage ... is always the product of a process", and in the case of visionOntv, some of the processes that produced its identity were those that fed videos from hosting platforms via RSS into the channels, since the kinds of videos that appeared on these channels were central to establishing its identity as a video activist group. However, the identity of an assemblage is "always precarious, since other processes ... can destabilize it" (DeLanda 2006b, 28), which in this case were the suspected maintenance or upgrading processes performed on the Blip platform by their engineers that caused inappropriate videos to be picked up by the RSS feed in question.

VisionOntv's response was to temporarily disable the offending RSS feed while they worked on a solution, which can be understood as a territorialization process to increase the internal homogeneity of the channels by excluding videos that were not consistent with visionOntv's identity as a video activist assemblage. The enrolment of this particular Blip feed therefore failed, and visionOntv had to work to find a solution that would allow it to be enrolled again.

This situation is also an example of what happens when an actor-network that was treated as a "black box" (Latour 1999, 185; Law 1992, 385) becomes unmasked because it no longer functions as expected. In such circumstances, it can no longer be treated as an "intermediary" (Latour 2005, 39), something that simply transports videos without changing them and remaining quietly in the background, but instead its complexity and specificity must be taken into account. With respect to this case, and drawing additionally upon the concepts of macro and micro assemblages, we see that the complexity of the Blip-RSS micro assemblage within the macro visionOntv assemblage could be ignored and treated as a simple, single actor, namely a video embedded in a web page, when it was delivering appropriate videos to the channel, but as soon as it stopped doing this, the black box had to be "opened up" and its complexity engaged with.

Another, more general example of the precariousness of hosting platform enrolment concerned the processes YouTube used to enforce copyright. These processes, which we saw in Chapter 2 were a common area of conflict between YouTube and its users (Lange 2017, 150–151), removed some videos from visionOntv's YouTube account and even threatened to close their whole account permanently because of perceived copyright violations. One such situation arose out of visionOntv's practice of sometimes uploading videos made by other activists onto their

YouTube channel. YouTube removed two of these videos at the request of the copyright holders of the music used in them, resulting in visionOntv's YouTube channel acquiring two "strikes".[2] VisionOntv, as a result, had become very cautious about uploading anything to YouTube that might contain copyright music and, after receiving the second strike, avoided doing so where they thought they would have problems, instead using other hosting services that they believed were less strict in this regard, such as Blip. Another example concerned a video they had on their channel by Adbusters, the anti-consumerist organization, which resulted in an infringement notice being issued by YouTube based on a complaint by the copyright holder of the video footage it used. While the video was initially take down by YouTube, visionOntv filed a counter-notice claiming fair use and the video was restored. We can see from these two examples that visionOntv had to work to maintain YouTube's enrolment in their assemblage by making editorial decisions about what they uploaded to it and also by responding to infringement notices. The editorial decisions can be understood as territorialization processes that homogenize the contents of visionOntv's YouTube account so that all the videos appearing on it comply with YouTube's terms of service with respect to copyright. Also, the filing of a counter-notice by visionOntv was a translation process, in that these are almost literally an "expression of a shared desire to arrive at the same result" (Callon 1980, 211), namely the distribution of copyright-compliant videos, as well as being an attempt, using Latour's (2005, 108) phrasing, to "induce" YouTube to "coexist" with visionOntv's assemblage.

What made these processes necessary was that YouTube, as an actor, was not a dutiful intermediary when it came to uploading videos to it so others could watch them, but was in fact a "mediator" (Latour 2005, 39), although its status as such was masked so long as visionOntv was uploading videos that did not trigger YouTube's copyright enforcement processes. While an actor in visionOntv's assemblage, YouTube was also an assemblage in its own right – a micro assemblage within visionOntv's macro assemblage – and therefore had its own challenges concerning stability, which gave rise to this conflict with visionOntv and other users. We can understand the processes it performed with respect to copyright, such as running algorithms to detect copyrighted material, providing copyright holders with a notification of any matches and a method to respond to them, and issuing copyright claim notices, as territorialization processes to homogenize the videos it hosted so that they were all complaint with copyright law. These processes therefore stabilized its identity as an assemblage that respected copyright, allowing it to coexist with copyright holders who might otherwise remove their content or sue YouTube (or its parent company), which were processes that threatened to destabilize it.

Enforcement of copyright was not the only source of visionOntv's concerns about the precariousness of their hosting services' enrolment. Another source of concern was that these hosting platforms could make changes to their business models that visionOntv would find unacceptable, such as charging subscription fees visionOntv was either unwilling or unable to pay or removing the RSS feature to force users to view the videos on the platforms' websites, enhancing their traffic and therefore attractiveness to advertisers, but preventing visionOntv from extracting videos from those platforms and feeding them into their own. Unlike the situation with copyright, however, visionOntv did not believe there would be processes open to them to translate the interests of these services to maintain their enrolment, and they would therefore have to detach those platforms from their assemblage in such circumstances. These hosting platforms were actors that visionOntv ultimately had a very limited ability to influence. Even where they did have some ability to influence them, such as with copyright counter-notices, the situation was still precarious. For example, an editorial error could lead to gaining a third "strike" from YouTube and, along with it, the closure of their account. On one occasion, VisionOntv had in fact thought this had happened to them when their YouTube account, comprising 800 videos at the time, was taken down without explanation, but then later restored without comment.

Therefore, because of this limited ability to influence these actors, no matter what processes visionOntv employed to maintain a particular platform's enrolment, there would be certain situations where they would be unable to either change decisions they found unacceptable or to prevent a platform from unilaterally detaching from their distribution assemblage, such as through the closure of their account or because the hosting platform itself had closed down. In response to the precariousness of this situation, visionOntv enrolled multiple video hosting platforms to provide redundant hosting of their videos in case the enrolment of one or more of them failed.[3] They used YouTube, Blip, Metacafe, and Dailymotion as their main hosting sites, but they also uploaded some of their videos to smaller video hosting services such as Vodpod and blinkx. Enrolling multiple hosting services stabilized their assemblage by providing redundant hosting of videos, but it also involved the additional work of uploading videos to the different platforms. This additional work was offset by enrolling another piece of Internet technology, OneLoad, which could simultaneously upload a video to multiple video hosting platforms. The use of redundant hosting platforms was also an acknowledgement that visionOntv's relationship with many of them would likely always be precarious since their interests ultimately diverged, with visionOntv pursuing "communicative freedom" in the face of the platforms' attempts to control and commodify this communication, which was a tension also experienced by other users of these platforms, as highlighted by, for example, Fenton (2012, 127–128) and Hess (2009, 426) in Chapter 2. This use of redundancy was in spite of the fact that visionOntv was able to successfully translate these interests into coexisting on a case-by-case basis most of the time.

The enrolment of VisionOntv's video production technologies within their distribution assemblage was precarious too, although for different reasons. VisionOntv were generally prepared to trade off video quality against increasing both quantity and turnaround time, believing their very limited resources were better used in creating more videos than editing existing footage. This meant, for instance, that visionOntv almost never edited any of their videos and simply uploaded the raw camera footage to save time, relying on different shooting formats and techniques to ensure the videos' coherence. One such technique was the use of the "pop-up studio" to conduct interviews, which was a precarious micro assemblage within the larger visionOntv macro assemblage. One configuration of the "pop-up studio" involved a laptop running the Wirecast software program, which took video feeds from two camcorders (a one-person shot of the interviewee and a two-person shot of the interviewee and interviewer), a microphone, and another laptop providing live cutaways of found footage, websites, or stills.[4] The operator of the laptop running Wirecast could select between the different feeds and decide which ones to use and mix together and whether to embed one feed within another. Wirecast in this configuration ran something like a virtual television studio control room, with the Wirecast operator in the role of the control room director.

However, because of the complexity of this configuration, and the fact that visionOntv relied on old, damaged, and makeshift hardware, demonstration and open source versions of software, and often inexperienced volunteers to assemble and run the studio on location, it sometimes did not run smoothly.[5] On these occasions, this configuration of the pop-up studio would prove difficult to set up or require repair and maintenance, sometimes resulting in disruption to the interview process. In such situations, it resembled Latour's example of the overhead projector breaking down during a lecture: "As the repairmen swarm around it, adjusting this lens, tightening that bulb, we remember that the projector is made of several parts, each with its role and function and its relatively independent goals ... In an instant our 'projector' grew from being composed of zero parts to one to many" (1999, 183). In Latour's example, the overhead projector could normally be considered a black box, and it was only during the exceptional circumstances of it breaking down that it was unmasked as an assemblage, requiring the opening of the black box to repair it. For the configuration of the pop-up studio considered here, though, the challenge was often black boxing it in the first place: It had to be assembled anew at each location in which it was used, and each of the components – tripods, cameras, microphones, lights, laptops, software, USB sound cards, gaffer tape, cables, volunteers, batteries, flash cards – had to be induced into coexisting again to mask its specificity so it would fade into the background and function as an intermediary in the interview process.

Facilitating Conversations: Strategies, Processes, and Difficulties

VisionOntv's venture was based on the belief that communities of social change could be fostered through conversations about the videos they distributed, and so they employed various strategies both to build audiences for these videos and to facilitate conversations within these audiences about them. One such strategy was to use multiple hosting platforms: Beyond providing redundancy, visionOntv believed this approach allowed them to attract a larger audience. While they acknowledged that YouTube attracted by far the largest online audience for non-professional videos, they also believed that their audience was not a mainstream one and that some of the smaller platforms may attract niche audiences more disposed to visionOntv's videos. For instance, they believed that Blip attracted a "more cultivated audience" than YouTube, and therefore thought that their videos might hold greater interest for the average Blip user. They found, however, that Blip was not suitable for audiences that were looking for immediate coverage of an event, as it could take up to 12 hours for a video to become available on its platform after uploading, and so visionOntv did not use it for rushes of unfolding situations, such as live demonstrations. VisionOntv were also using platforms other than YouTube to attract audiences because they were concerned that it did not give due prominence to their videos. They believed that those who could afford to pay to have their videos feature in search results and in recommendations, such as commercial media organizations, were taking audiences away from those who could not, which was a position similar to the one adopted by some early YouTube users during the Oprah controversy discussed in Chapter 2.

The commercial, legal, technical, and editorial considerations visionOntv made with regard to which hosting platforms to enrol, how they went about enrolling them, and the measures they took to maintain their enrolment, both with regard to building audiences and increasing the stability of their assemblages, reflect the platforms' status as mediators whose individual specificity had to be engaged with, adapted, and adapted to, rather than simple intermediaries whose functioning could be taken for granted. Similar to Lange's (2017, 150–151) observation from Chapter 2 that "finding a place of distributive purity online is … difficult", visionOntv were unable to find a hosting platform whose interests completely aligned with theirs, and therefore they resorted to a strategy that used an ensemble of hosting platforms to pursue these interests. While this general strategy was initially successful, we will see in the last section that it eventually ran into difficulties.

While visionOntv used different video hosting platforms to enrol audiences, they were not interested in facilitating discussions about their videos in the comments sections of any of them. One reason for this was similar to the views of Juhasz (2008, 305–306) and Hess (2009, 412) from Chapter 2: VisionOntv did not believe that the comments sections of these platforms were places for generating discursive communities around their videos. They believed that the platforms were primarily about entertainment, and therefore often attracted "low quality" and "empty" comments, and that activist videos in particular were targets for "ranters" and "trolls" generating unconstructive conflict.

Instead of facilitating conversations about their videos on the hosting platforms, visionOntv used the videos on these platforms to attempt to enrol audiences within their Liferay platform, which they believed was a more suitable platform for the kinds of conversations they desired. They did this by including a link to the Liferay channel in the description section of the video that related to the video's genre. For example, a video critical of Facebook and Twitter from an activist perspective on visionOntv's YouTube channel contained a link in the description to the "Plug and Play" channel on Liferay, which was for activist videos related to current trends in technology. The video, the description, and the link were all actants, amongst others, that worked together to enrol audiences within the Liferay platform: A casual viewer might, for instance, be intrigued enough by the video to read the description and click on the link, as opposed to playing another video or doing something else. Translations in this situation involved "channelling people in different directions" (Latour 1987, 117), and the agency of the assemblage to translate the interests of the audience member in this way, and move them in a different direction, was a property of the "web of materialised relations" of which they were a part: Neither the audience member, YouTube, the video, the description pane, the link, Liferay, or the various visionOntv members and volunteers acted alone in the enrolment process; rather, they acted "in relation to other actors, lined up with them" (Law and Mol 2008, 58).

VisionOntv's Facebook and Twitter accounts were also used to enrol users into their platform. They did this by using these social media platforms to announce new videos as they became available online, typically by embedding links to the relevant Liferay channel in their posts. As with the video hosting platforms, visionOntv did not try and generate discussions about the videos on these social media platforms, as they did not believe that they were conducive to fostering the kinds of conversations that could eventually lead to the formation of communities of social change. One reason for this was that they perceived the comments on these platforms as ephemeral: Only conversations attached to the most recent posts were presented to the user through the feed on their home page, with the rest quickly disappearing from easy access, which was exacerbated by the fact that Internet search engines were not indexing these posts at the time. Another reason concerned the lack of appropriateness of corporate-owned sites as places to conduct and archive discussions about social change, which was also part of visionOntv's reasoning for not using the comments sections of the video hosting platforms for this purpose and reflected similar concerns expressed by others in Chapter 2 (Costanza-Chock 2008; Presence 2015, 193).

These processes visionOntv engaged in with respect to commenting on the social networking and video hosting platforms can be analysed in terms of the concept of territorialization. VisionOntv enforced a norm to ensure that only the components of these technologies that were consistent with its identity as an assemblage to foster social change were included within it: YouTube's functionality allowing video hosting, syndication of those videos via RSS, and the inclusion of html links in descriptions and Facebook's and Twitter's functionality allowing html links to be included in posts were all included because they were seen as consistent with this identity, since they could be used to send audiences to a platform where visionOntv believed appropriate conversations could take place. On the other hand, the commenting functionality on these platforms was not seen as facilitating the right kind of conversations and was therefore excluded. In this situation, visionOntv therefore treated YouTube, Facebook, and Twitter as assemblages of components, rather than as black boxed, single actors, applying sorting processes to them that excluded the components visionOntv considered inconsistent with its identity.

The Facebook and Twitter posts announcing videos were actants of a similar kind to the video-description-link assemblages just discussed in relation to YouTube, and they had the same purpose: They were actants used by visionOntv to "channel" Facebook and Twitter users onto visionOntv's platform by transforming a user's interest in, for instance, continuing to browse posts on their home page news feed into one resulting in clicking on the link in visionOntv's post. These enrolment attempts were, however, subject to various processes that caused them to fail in some cases. One such process involved the Facebook algorithms that decided whether a post would be sent to a friend's news feed or not, which prevented at least some of visionOntv's posts from reaching all their friends' accounts. Similarly, as already discussed above in relation to using these platforms with respect to conversations, a constant flow of posts in friends' and followers' feeds meant that even some of visionOntv's posts that were received were not seen.

While visionOntv had some success generating traffic on their platform through these strategies, they were generally unsuccessful in getting users who arrived there to use the various Liferay tools designed to generate audience interaction and conversation. These tools included functionality for commenting on videos, a bulletin board, a wiki, and text chat functionality. This lack of success was in spite of visionOntv's attempts to stimulate discussions through seeding topics and responding to the few users that used these tools. VisionOntv believed that these communication tools were not being used because they were not user friendly. To help facilitate user interaction on their platform, visionOntv had attempted to upgrade Liferay to a new version that contained "OpenSocial", a framework that provided more flexible and more user-friendly communication tools than the pre-existing tools. However, the upgrade process had not gone smoothly, and they were not able to complete it successfully during the 2011/12 phase of the fieldwork. This situation frustrated visionOntv's plans, as it delayed their advance to the next stage of their platform's development and therefore prevented them from advancing toward their overall objective.

This upgrade process can be analysed as a failed territorialization of visionOntv's assemblage: It was an attempt to separate a component from it that was not consistent with visionOntv's desired identity as a platform for facilitating conversations, namely the pre-existing Liferay communication tools, and to replace it with the new OpenSocial component that was. It can also be analysed as a failed translation process: Upgrading Liferay so as to replace the pre-existing, difficult to use communications tools with OpenSocial was a failed attempt at "creating convergences" (Callon 1980, 211) between Liferay and visionOntv's audience, an unsuccessful attempt at inducing them to coexist.

One main reason this process failed was visionOntv's inability to translate the interests of Liferay, an assemblage of people, technologies, and other components itself, into something more aligned with their own. This manifested specifically in the difficulty they faced in getting technical support from Liferay's staff to help with the upgrade. VisionOntv used the free "Community Edition", which did not come with support, unlike the "Enterprise Edition", which came with support but required the payment of a licence fee. VisionOntv were not, however, prepared to pay the licence fee because they were committed to their platform being free to operate, both because of their very limited budget, but also because they believed this would help entice other video activist groups to adopt it (which will be discussed in detail in the fourth section). Framing this situation in terms of Callon's (1986) formulation of the translation process, VisionOntv's negotiations with Liferay's staff to obtain the support they needed failed to change that organization's problematization of the platform as ultimately a commercial entity, and therefore the only strategy that remained open to visionOntv was to accept Liferay's problematization and pay the licence fee, which they were not prepared to do, and so the interests of the two parties could not be aligned.

Supporting Salovaara's (2015, 13–14) observation that the agency of assemblages which are part of media ecosystems "is a distributed phenomenon that can only be understood by tracing the complex ecologies" of those ecosystems, we have seen that the restricted agency of visionOntv's assemblage to generate conversations is understandable from an examination of the relationships that existed between the different human and technological components of the media ecology of which it was a part: Overall, visionOntv were unable to facilitate conversations on Liferay because of inadequate tools and their inability to upgrade those tools, and declined to do so on social media and video hosting sites as visionOntv did not believe these were appropriate places for this kind of activity. This situation, coupled with their inability to use torrent technology to create a screening network and their belief that video hosting platforms were unsuitable for this, left visionOntv frustrated with respect to their overall objective of facilitating conversations that could lead to the emergence of communities of social change. In short, this restricted agency of visionOntv's assemblage can be understood as an emergent property of the interactions between its components, human and technological, following DeLanda's (2010, 68) observation that "the properties and capacities of a whole emerge from the causal interactions between its parts".

Volunteers and the Translation of Interests

In addition to visionOntv's core team, which consisted of the founders Hamish and Richard introduced in Chapter 2 and one other person who was temporarily involved with the venture during the 2011/12 fieldwork, many other people worked at visionOntv as part-time volunteers. While these volunteers greatly increased visionOntv's capacity, the relationships also proved problematic. The process for becoming a volunteer at visionOntv was a very informal one, and it usually simply required someone asking to become involved in the venture, although sometimes people were approached by the core team to help with specific projects. There were around 10 people that the core team regularly called upon to help with projects, such as filming at conferences or helping with running training workshops, and there were around another 15 loosely associated people who helped moderate the visionOntv channels and who became involved in its activities on an ad hoc basis.

The problematic aspect of these relationships stemmed from failed translations of interests. A specific example of this relates to the RSS problem discussed in the first section: VisionOntv believed the main reason this was so difficult to resolve was their failure on several occasions to translate the interests of technically skilled volunteers into ones that would help visionOntv solve the problem at hand. They believed that skilled technicians who were inclined towards volunteering on activist projects were only interested in solving technical problems that they found challenging, but that this particular problem was relatively straightforward, although time-consuming, for a skilled technician. This meant that the volunteers they used were either not sufficiently skilled to solve the problem, or would only solve the problem in a way that they found interesting, but which in the end did not meet visionOntv's specific needs. This latter case highlights two aspects of enrolment processes in general that make them precarious and that can lead to their failure: Law's (2003, 2009, 144) point, made in somewhat melodramatic terms, that interests are not always translated with fidelity, but can in fact involve "betrayal". The second aspect concerns Law and Mol's observation that "to act is not to master, for the results of what is being done are often unexpected" (2008, 58): The visionOntv core team, in acting to enrol volunteer technicians to solve their problem, were not in fact masters of the situation.

More generally, visionOntv's inability to translate the volunteers' longer-term interests into something that they could offer meant that the enrolment of volunteers was typically short-lived, with few people staying involved for more than one year. Reasons for this included the fact that visionOntv had no money to pay volunteers, which meant that financially remunerative work would eventually draw volunteers away once found. Similarly, the volunteers did not see visionOntv as a significant addition to their CVs because it was not a known brand, and therefore other opportunities that could add to their professional profile eventually took precedence. Finally, there were few social ties to hold volunteers to the venture. These ties generally did not form because the volunteers' involvement with visionOntv, and their interaction with each other, was sporadic and because visionOntv's platform was not yet functioning as a place to foster communities, as we saw above. Tensions between actors' short-term and long-term interests that result in enrolments failing have also been identified in other ANT studies, a notable example being Callon's (1986) St. Brieuc Bay case study from Chapter 3, where researchers were only temporarily able to translate the fishermen's long-term interests in restocking the bay with scallops into an attitude that denied their short-term interest in fishing the bay for immediate profit.

The enrolments of some of the longer-term volunteers also proved precarious, and this went beyond matters concerning the general financial, professional, and social interests discussed above. For example, one such volunteer had become uncomfortable with visionOntv's increasing focus on "citizen journalism", as this was not a form of activist video he was interested in, preferring to make more "polished" documentaries instead. Another long-term volunteer had become uncomfortable with the quality of visionOntv's output, due to its reliance on volunteers with minimal training, its use of makeshift equipment, and its emphasis on rapid production turnaround to maximize quantity.

These diverging interests had led to these two volunteers drifting away from visionOntv and concentrating more on their own video activist projects, which meant that their enrolment within the assemblage was becoming increasingly precarious.

While the reworking of interests is one possible response to a failed enrolment (Callon and Law 1982, 620), visionOntv had little scope to rework either their or their volunteers' different interests because of limited financial resources, the specific nature of the venture, and their commitment to a certain way of working. Instead, visionOntv's response to their general inability to maintain volunteers for the longer term was to accept the precarious and short-term nature of these enrolments, meaning that visionOntv's core members were involved in ongoing processes of enrolling volunteers into the venture and training them. These processes were both directly and indirectly about maintaining the stability of the assemblage: directly, in that there were some critical processes in the assemblage that the core team were unable to perform themselves (such as specific technical tasks, like the RSS feed implementation), and indirectly in that volunteers freed up the core team to concentrate on other tasks and push the venture towards its goals while their commitment to it lasted.

The training of volunteers can also be seen as a territorialization process to maintain the identity of visionOntv's assemblage by "increasing its degree of internal homogeneity" (DeLanda 2006b, 12): It was partly meant to ensure that the volunteers adhered to visionOntv's processes and principles, instilling in them such things as a commitment to visionOntv's way of making videos and to continuing the development of the visionOntv platform using open source software and standards. The reason for impressing upon volunteers this latter commitment relates to visionOntv's plans to use their platform as the basis for a wider network of video activist groups beyond their own, which is examined in the next section.

Building the Video Activist Macro Assemblage

In addition to creating and distributing activist videos online, visionOntv also tried to develop their platform as a model for other video activists to adopt as another way of achieving their purpose of fostering communities of social change. Their ambition was to connect up the different video activist groups operating in the UK and elsewhere into a broader network, sharing videos, audiences, and conversations within it. They believed that visionOntv, and these other groups, would be more effective in promoting social change if they were able to support each other's activities, rather than operating as isolated, individual efforts.

To help bring this about, visionOntv were developing their platform as an open one, using both open source software and open standards. They believed that using open source software and standards would ensure interoperability between the different video activist projects that adopted their model in the future, allowing content and data to be easily shared between them. They were also developing the platform using software that was free, which they believed would help its adoption amongst activists with little or no access to funds. When different activist groups eventually adopted their platform, visionOntv saw themselves becoming just one interconnected node within this open activist network, which would not be owned or controlled by any of the individual nodes. VisionOntv's development of their platform with open source software and standards, and the promotion of it as a model for others to adopt, can be partly understood as a territorialization process: It was an attempt to facilitate the creation and ensure the stability of the larger network they envisioned by making each of the nodes within it homogenous, where the nodes can be understood as micro assemblages and the larger network itself as a macro assemblage. VisionOntv's activities here are analogous in some important respects to DeLanda's (2006b, 82) example in Chapter 3 of the non-spatial territorialization processes that organizations such as trade and industry associations perform to integrate the activities of the US computer manufacturing industry, such as the setting of technological standards. VisionOntv's plans were, however, being frustrated by the various complications in developing their platform discussed in the above sections, as they were reluctant to vigorously promote their platform as a model until it was fully functional and stable.

In addition to their plans to create the nodes in this future video activist network by promoting their platform to other activist groups, visionOntv also organized and ran workshops to train people in how to make and distribute activist videos, as well as helping the participants organize into self-sustaining groups so that they could eventually become nodes within this network. These workshops were promoted as the "Making News Roadshow" and were described as a series of free "citizen TV reporter workshops" that emphasized helping participants get their videos made and distributed quickly and easily (visionOntv 2011). Participants were not required to have any video making experience, and any video recording equipment could be used, including camera phones. The workshops were typically only one or two days in duration, and therefore this gave visionOntv very limited time in which to train participants to make videos.

To be able to provide effective video production training for beginners in a short period of time, visionOntv relied on templates to simplify and accelerate the workshop teaching process. They had developed three different templates for participants to use: The "street report", which was the shortest format video and was 30 seconds to one minute in duration and comprised a single shot. These were made by one person, typically just using the video camera on their phone, and were uploaded unedited to the Internet. Another template was for an animated, video slideshow using still images and the free Animoto video creation web application, which allowed people without any camera equipment to participate too. The final template was the video news report, which was a quick turn-around two- to three-minute video using a camcorder. These templates were a distillation of the core team's video making experience and were designed to allow new video producers to quickly learn how to make videos of acceptable quality that could be ready for uploading to the Internet in a few hours at the most. The templates formed the core of the workshops, where visionOntv would explain and demonstrate their use and set the participants various exercises using them. Small leaflets explaining and graphically illustrating each template were made available at the workshops as reminders, and electronic versions of these were also available on the visionOntv platform (visionOntv 2013).

The templates were an important part of the enrolment and stabilization process for these potential new nodes: VisionOntv believed that the templates led to higher quality videos being made than would otherwise be possible, which would both encourage the producer to upload them and increase their likelihood of attracting an audience. Also, the simplification and compression of the production processes enabled by the templates meant that it was more likely that a video would be completed, rather than remaining work-in-progress in a camera or on a hard drive because the producer did not have the time or expertise to complete it. These templates can be analysed as actants, used by visionOntv's facilitators at the workshops to enrol participants into the wider, macro assemblage: The use of these mediators was part of visionOntv's effort to translate the participants' interest in producing activist videos into something consistent with visionOntv's interest in creating a sustainable node. This situation can also be analysed as a "coding" process (DeLanda 2010, 13), where language, both in the form of the verbal and printed description of the templates, was used to attempt to fix the identity of the nodes emerging from the workshops.

In addition to teaching participants how to use the templates, the Making News Roadshow workshops also showed them how to use visionOntv's platform as a place to set up and organize their own video activist group. An example of how they went about this comes from a weekend workshop conducted in Liverpool in June 2011. This workshop, involving around 25 participants, concentrated on teaching visionOntv's video templates, as discussed above, but also involved a session on how to upload videos to the Internet, as well as one explaining the functionality of visionOntv's platform, which also included instructions on how to link an RSS feed from the participants' YouTube accounts into it. There was a section set up within the visionOntv platform for this, where the workshop group was dubbed the "Merseyside Street Reporters Network" (MSRN). The longer-term plan was for this section of the platform to be spun off as a separate node of the nascent network, once the group had reached a critical mass and stabilized.

Overall, the Making News Roadshow can be analysed as a territorialization process focused on forming and stabilizing the identity of the macro assemblage by creating micro assemblages from the different workshop groups by not only teaching them production and distribution skills, but also by instilling in them a shared commitment to visionOntv's particular production and distribution practices (this latter aspect being analogous to the creation of behavioural norms by professional associations in DeLanda's (2006b, 82) computer industry example). Aspects of this process were proving problematic however, and frustrating the formation of the macro assemblage.

For example, the MSRN only stabilized temporarily as a micro assemblage and had mostly dissipated six months after the workshop. One reason for this was the difficulty in using Liferay's communication tools, as discussed earlier. In fact, the MSRN members only used these tools for the first month after the workshop, primarily to request help with technical issues regarding how to use aspects of the platform, in spite of the core members' attempts to stimulate discussions using them. In response to these difficulties with Liferay, one of visionOntv's volunteers, who was also a workshop participant, set up an MSRN Facebook group during this first month. Soon after this, one of visionOntv's core members posted to the Facebook group encouraging the MSRN members to continue using the tools on the section of Liferay set up for them, but this appeared to have had no effect as the Facebook group took over as the primary place for MSRN online interactions.

This situation can be analysed into a series of territorialization and deterritorialization processes contesting the stability of the macro assemblage: After the initial territorialization process of the workshop, which formed the MSRN within the macro assemblage, the establishment of the MSRN Facebook group was a deterritorialization process that destabilized the assemblage because it increased its internal heterogeneity by introducing a communication tool that had different characteristics from the Liferay platform (for example, it was neither open source, nor interoperable with Liferay). This threatened the stability of the nascent macro assemblage since, as Deleuze notes, "the assemblage's only unity is that of co-functioning" component parts (Deleuze and Parnet 2006, 52), and the loss of interoperability ("co-functioning") caused by adopting Facebook over Liferay undermined that unity. The core member's Facebook post was an unsuccessful territorialization process attempting to reduce the macro assemblage's heterogeneity to preserve its unity.[6]

This situation is similar to Rivera and Cox's (2016) ANT study of the failed attempt to form an online community around a collaborative technology platform at a Mexican University, discussed in Chapter 3, and can also be analysed in terms of translations of interests as was done with that study: The introduction of the Liferay platform to the workshop's participants reflected visionOntv's core team's interest in creating a macro assemblage with certain properties, which for them offset its inadequacies as a communication platform at the time. The session at the workshop on how to use visionOntv's platform, the core team member's Facebook post, and the Liferay platform's functionality and usability were, however, unable to translate the workshop participants' interest in communicating with each other into something consistent with the platform's use as their primary communication tool.

While the Facebook group took over as the main place the MSRN communicated online, activity on it reduced over time, and had nearly ceased around six months after it was set up. Similarly, while the group began holding monthly meetings in local venues in Liverpool just after the workshop, these stopped after around five months. Finally, within the same time period, video uploads from the MSRN had mostly ceased. While the communication difficulties arising from the use of Liferay destabilized the MSRN in the first few weeks of its existence, these did not have a significant impact once the transition to the Facebook group was made, and so were not a direct cause of its demise. The cause was instead partly due to circumstances specific to individual MSRN members, and these resulted in their enrolment within it failing. The following analysis of two workshop participants, Greg and "Sophie" (pseudonym), illustrates the kinds of circumstances involved.

Greg's enrolment within the MSRN failed because the various processes that maintained it either ceased during the first six months after the workshop or did not prove effective enough to maintain it. One example of this concerned the local MSRN meetings. Greg saw the MSRN as primarily an offline group that used online tools to organize and maintain momentum between meetings, and although he had taken the lead in setting up these meetings, ill health had prevented him from continuing with this. Since no one else was willing or able to step in and organize the meetings, this monthly process for maintaining his enrolment ceased. Facebook also proved an inadequate tool to maintain his enrolment, as he felt overwhelmed by the large volume of notifications he received on it daily, and so mostly ignored ones that were not an immediate priority.

Finally, the process he used to distribute his videos was problematic, and ultimately failed, resulting in them no longer appearing on visionOntv's platform: Greg uploaded his videos to YouTube and linked them to the visionOntv platform using an RSS feed. This was done at the workshop by a facilitator and used his son's YouTube account because Greg didn't want to go to the effort at the time of setting up his own account. However, some time later, Greg's son wanted to reclaim his YouTube account, and upon doing so made it private, which meant that Greg's videos no longer appeared on the visionOntv platform. While Greg had immediately set up his own YouTube account after handing the other one back, he didn't know how to change the RSS feed, which meant that for some months none of his videos were appearing on the visionOntv platform, although he eventually received some assistance with this and resolved the problem. By the time the situation had eventually resolved, however, he did not have the commitment or energy, due to illness, to upload the old videos to his new account or to continue making new videos.

Sophie's enrolment within the MSRN also failed mainly because of reasons unique to her circumstances. Her primary motivation for being involved in the MSRN was to make and distribute her own activist videos, rather than to view other people's videos or become involved in online discussions. She stopped making videos around two months after the workshop, however, when she lost her mobile phone, which was her only video-making tool, halting the primary process that was maintaining her enrolment within the MSRN. It took nearly 12 months before she was able to afford another video-capable phone, which caused her a loss of momentum with respect to her involvement in the MSRN, and as a result, she stopped attending the Liverpool meetings. She also rarely visited the MSRN Facebook group during this period: Her usual motivation for engaging with Facebook groups was seeing posts from them on her personal Facebook feed, but the MSRN posts were not appearing there, mostly likely due to the combined effect of Facebook's post-filtering algorithms and the small number of posts actually made on the MSRN page. By the time she had bought her new video-capable phone and was ready to recommence making videos, the MSRN had become inactive.

Both Greg and Sophie's enrolment within the MSRN was maintained by a precarious network of diverse actants, and although these actants were the same (or at least of the same type) in both cases, some faded into the background as intermediaries for one of them, while for the other they were mediators whose specificity had to be attended to. In Sophie's case, for example, the fact that video-making equipment is relatively expensive to replace was a major reason why her enrolment with the MSRN failed, while for Greg it had no immediate relevance to his situation.

In addition to the specific situations of individual participants like those of Greg and Sophie, there were also other, more general factors that prevented the MSRN from forming into a stable assemblage. One such factor was that the visionOntv macro assemblage lacked the top-down emergent properties that could have helped stabilize the MSRN micro assemblage: Unlike the examples in Chapter 3 where emergent properties provided cohesiveness to nomad armies and interpersonal networks (DeLanda 2010, 68–69, 2016, 10–11), the difficulty the visionOntv platform had in enrolling users, and the fact that the macro assemblage did not contain at the time any other active micro assemblages (that is, other video activist groups), meant that there were insufficient interactions within the macro assemblage to create top-down emergent properties that might have stabilized the MSRN.

Also, while the Making News Roadshow workshops were relatively expensive and time-consuming events to prepare and run, a single weekend workshop with only online follow up and support was insufficient to territorialize a disparate collection of people with little or no video-making experience into an assemblage that was fluent in the use of the templates and the visionOntv platform and that also shared a commitment to using that platform as their primary online space. Unlike the nomadic cavalry teams discussed in Chapter 3, where intensive training led to teams having emergent properties that normalized team members' behaviour while also providing resources for those members, the territorialization and coding processes of the workshop were insufficient to create these emergent properties.

Overall, this meant visionOntv's core team were heavily involved in supporting and maintaining the MSRN for some time after the workshop. However, they were not able to commit the amount of time necessary to keep the group from dwindling in number or to help it recruit more members so it could reach a critical mass where properties might emerge that could stabilize it for the longer term. While visionOntv acknowledged all these factors, and the fact that their attempt to establish the MSRN as a micro assemblage was premature, they considered the Liverpool workshop a success because they learnt something about the workshop and node-building process and because it resulted in a significant number of activist videos being added to visionOntv's platform, in spite of the fact that the MSRN did not flourish into a self-sustaining entity.

The Changing Identity of visionOntv's Assemblage

Returning to visionOntv five years later, I found that various destabilization processes, some of which had their origins in the processes discussed in the previous sections, had eventually led them to reassess their goals and operations. One consequence of these processes was that visionOntv was no longer focused on developing its platform as a place to facilitate conversations. This decision was partly based on the belief that Liferay was ultimately unable to compete with corporate social media platforms for users' attention: Even with the OpenSocial upgrade, visionOntv believed that from a user's perspective, Liferay looked and functioned like a "geek project", whereas platforms like Facebook were seen as "shiny" and "fashionable", with superior functionality, usability, and ascetics. This problem was compounded by the fact that the Liferay organization no longer provided upgrades for the free "Community Edition", while (free) corporate social media platforms were receiving regular updates. In addition, visionOntv did not believe any of the alternative open source social media platforms that they might use instead of Liferay offered a better solution because they felt the development of such platforms had stalled because the growing dominance of Facebook and other corporate social media platforms had discouraged open source developers from working in this area.

Callon and Latour (1981, 284) analyse competitive situations such as these in terms of the number of human and non-human entities that the competing actors can enrol, where the one that enrols the largest number of these "creates greatness and longevity making the others small and provisional in comparison". Applying this to the platforms above, Facebook as an organization had vast human and material resources at its disposal that were focused on providing free, engaging, social media software to users, while the Liferay organization not only had a small fraction of Facebook's resources, but these resources were also not primarily focused on developing social media tools for the free Community Edition.[7]

VisionOntv also continued to believe that corporate social media platforms were unsuitable places to facilitate the kinds of conversations they wanted, but changes to those platforms over the intervening years had meant that they were also proving increasingly inadequate in driving audiences to Liferay. For example, visionOntv believed that only a small number of people who "liked" their Facebook page were actually receiving the posts they were making to it, and while this had been an issue for them during 2011/12, as discussed above, they believed that the numbers had decreased even further over the intervening years. Facebook in fact acknowledged the decline in "organic reach" during this period, which they defined as "how many people you can reach for free on Facebook by posting to your Page", and attributed it to how its algorithms handled the increase in traffic over this period (Boland 2014). The way Facebook's algorithmic processes had responded to this increase in traffic had therefore made VisionOntv's posts even less effective actants in the user enrolment process than they had been previously.

Facebook offered a territorialization process in the form of its "boost a post" functionality that helped counter the deterritorialization brought about by their algorithmic actants. This functionality allowed users to increase the reach of their posts by paying to have it appear in more users' news feeds than it would otherwise (Facebook 2016). VisionOntv, however, did not adopt this stabilizing counter process, not only because of the very limited funds the venture had at its disposal, but also because they believed paying to include this functionality as a component within their assemblage would further intensify the contradiction that they as anti-capitalist activists committed to open source software experienced when using a capitalist, closed source platform like Facebook, and they were concerned that increasing the heterogeneity of their assemblage in this way would further destabilize its identity.

Instead of enrolling Facebook's "boost a post" functionality as an actant to stabilize their assemblage, visionOntv enrolled a different actant, Buffer, which was a social media management tool. While the work involved in uploading to multiple social media platforms meant that visionOntv's use of platforms other than Facebook and Twitter had hitherto been sporadic, Buffer enabled them to post simultaneously to visionOntv's accounts on Facebook, Twitter, Google+, and LinkedIn. In spite of this increased distribution activity, visionOntv had noticed a decline in its audience since the 2011/12 fieldwork period, with a noticeable downward trend in views for their more recent videos. VisionOntv believed that the increasing limitations of Liferay and corporate social media as actants for enrolling audiences into their assemblage had contributed to this downward trend, although they also suspected that their videos were not being promoted by YouTube's recommendation and search algorithms as much as they had been previously.

Therefore, given the limitations of Liferay and commercial social media, and the lack of suitable open source alternatives, visionOntv believed they did not have adequate tools to enrol, maintain, and engage users in sufficient numbers to allow their assemblage to develop the desired emergent property of becoming a stable space for facilitating communities of social change. Furthermore, because they believed that it was unlikely that this situation would change in the near term, given the continued dominance of corporate social media, visionOntv decided to abandon this goal and focus their efforts elsewhere. This meant that during the 2016/17 fieldwork period, visionOntv were no longer actively developing their platform or trying to drive traffic to it, nor were they focused on producing videos, since these weren't needed to seed conversations on the platform, and they were also not receiving sufficient views to warrant the production effort.

Instead of developing their platform, producing videos, and trying to enrol audiences, visionOntv's main focus during the 2016/17 fieldwork was on developing the macro assemblage, albeit in a new form that they dubbed "The Open Media Network" (OMN). The OMN was still in the early stages of development during this period, but it was planned as a reworking of the macro assemblage concept discussed in the previous section: The OMN, like the earlier macro assemblage concept, was to be an interoperable network of different activists' websites, although one main difference was that it would not be based on different activist groups adopting visionOntv's platform, but rather each activist group would use their own website or platform. These would, however, all include a webpage, section, or sidebar that drew content from an RSS feed. This RSS feed would be an aggregation of RSS feeds from other activist groups in the OMN. VisionOntv had progressed as far as developing a very basic prototype of the OMN RSS feed by the end of the 2016/17 fieldwork.

VisionOntv planned to publish a standardized list of tags for the micro assemblages that would eventually join the OMN. It was envisaged that the micro assemblages would tag the content they produced with them and that they would also use these tags to filter the OMN RSS feed to ensure that it was relevant for them. The tags in the prototype were words and phrases (such as "hate crimes", "public sector cuts", and "kurds"), and therefore the future publication and adoption of this list, if it were to occur, would be part of a coding process, using language to stabilize the macro assemblage: Without a common set of tags, each of the micro assemblages would not know how to label the content they produced so it could be accurately filtered by the other micro assemblages within the OMN receiving the RSS feed, which could lead to various problems, such as irrelevant or even inappropriate content appearing on their sites. Such a situation could destabilize the macro assemblage, or even prevent it from forming in the first place, as it could lead to micro assemblages within the OMN deciding to discontinue the feed's use because its content was destabilizing their identity, or it could discourage those who might join from taking the feed at all for the same reason.[8]

The development of an aggregated RSS feed was part of the original visionOntv project, but this was in fact the element of the problematic RSS implementation discussed in the first section that remained intractable during the 2011/12 fieldwork despite the multiple attempts to resolve it. VisionOntv did, however, make an important step towards resolving this issue during the 2016/17 phase of the fieldwork, having eventually found a willing volunteer programmer who wrote some software code that allowed visionOntv to create the prototype. There was, however, still an enormous amount of work to be done before the RSS feed was ready for public release, including testing, feedback, and additional software coding leading to the development of alpha and beta versions, the development of a user interface, the support for multi-tagging and Boolean logic to allow for customized filtering, amongst other things. Beyond that there was also the work involved in fixing bugs and providing upgrades once it was released, as well as the work involved in enrolling, and maintaining the enrolment, of the other activist micro assemblages. This situation highlights Latour's observation concerning the centrality of work in the formation of actor-networks (Gane 2004, 83), and therefore the importance, in some situations at least, of the disparity between the number of human and non-human actors available to activist media groups to perform such work compared to established media, and hence their significant competitive disadvantage in spite of the availability of free to use software and relatively inexpensive Internet connectivity.

To improve the OMN's chance of success, visionOntv had planned to include activist groups other than those who were primarily engaged in creating video to join, such as those whose online content was mostly text-based, unlike their earlier conception of the macro assemblage. This, they believed, would increase the likelihood of the macro assemblage eventually growing to a sufficient scale, and having a sufficient "density of connections" (DeLanda 2016, 10), to allow properties to emerge that would stabilize it into a self-sustaining entity. Also, with this much larger pool of potential activist groups to draw from, visionOntv would be able to focus on enrolling pre-existing activist groups into the OMN, rather than continuing to pursue the Making News Roadshow process of node formation, greatly reducing the work involved in creating the macro assemblage.

With their focus on the OMN, visionOntv's platform became less central to their venture. Rather than being a place for conversation and an exemplar for others to adopt, its role now was simply as visionOntv's node within the planned OMN. As a result, visionOntv maintained it as a functioning platform, but did not have plans to develop it further, at least not until after the OMN was operational. This led to some compromises in its operation that increased its precariousness. One such compromise concerned video hosting. As we saw earlier, visionOntv uploaded their videos to multiple hosting platforms, with YouTube and Blip being their main platforms, using OneLoad to offset the additional work involved by uploading to several of these sites at once. This situation had changed considerably by the time of the 2016/17 fieldwork: OneLoad had changed its pricing plan in 2014 so that the free aspects that visionOntv had been using became prohibitively expensive for them, and so they stopped using it. They had also decided that the benefits derived from having their videos on multiple sites did not offset the extra work required to upload to each hosting platform individually, and so they only uploaded to YouTube and Blip after they stopped using OneLoad, as this still provided visionOntv with some redundancy and audience diversity.

Blip closed down in 2015, however, and so visionOntv were only hosting on YouTube by the time of the 2016/17 fieldwork. In fact, their reliance on YouTube at this point not only concerned hosting, but also extended to aggregation, as the Participatory Culture Foundation had stopped supporting and distributing Miro Community: In the absence of Miro Community, visionOntv started using YouTube's playlists to aggregate videos for each of the channels within their platform, embedding the appropriate playlist into each of the Liferay channel pages. This sole reliance on YouTube made visionOntv's platform more precarious, although the situation was far less threatening to their venture than it would have been in 2011/12.

One reason for this was based on visionOntv's belief that YouTube's attitude towards copyright had become "gentler": They had not received any takedown notices from YouTube since the 2011/12 fieldwork, although they had experienced some videos being muted or blocked in some countries, but this had not earned visionOntv any additional strikes, and their previous strikes had expired. Another, more important reason was that the YouTube playlists embedded within Liferay were merely placeholders until the OMN could be launched, when they would be replaced by the aggregated RSS feed. While visionOntv still wanted to maintain videos on their platform, and for their YouTube audience, to give them an online presence until the OMN RSS feed was operational, this was not critical to their venture. In fact, although visionOntv intended to keep their YouTube channel as a secondary platform for their videos once the OMN was launched, they did not envisage YouTube playing a role within the OMN. This was because the OMN RSS feed required video files to be tagged and have metadata (such as comments) attached to them, and this was not possible with YouTube. Any videos visionOntv wanted to include within the OMN would have to be uploaded (from the offline backups they kept) to another hosting services that allowed this. Therefore, if YouTube closed down visionOntv's account or ceased operations, while this would be very inconvenient, it would not impact the development of the OMN, or the future role of visionOntv's platform within it.

Even though the enrolment of multiple actors within visionOntv's 2011/12 assemblage had failed by 2016/17, such as OneLoad, Blip, and Miro Community, and in spite of the fact that the stability of the 2016/17 assemblage had become heavily reliant on a previously problematic actor, visionOntv did not consider the work required to increase its stability (such as uploading their videos to a redundant hosting platform) a priority because, in its current configuration, visionOntv's micro assemblage was only of temporary value.

Overall, in spite of the various changes visionOntv underwent between 2011/12 and 2016/17 discussed above, the resulting changes to its identity over that period were more a matter of degree rather than kind, since the deterritorialization processes it had undergone in the intervening years are best understood as "relative" rather than "absolute", which we can see through an analysis of the situation using DeLanda's (2006b, 30, 123–124) concept of assemblage diagrams. While a detailed diagrammatic analysis would require a Weberian-style treatment of activist organizations similar to the one DeLanda draws upon to define the axes of the diagram for hierarchical organizations in his example (2006b, 30), which is beyond our scope here, using the concept of diagrams to frame these changes in more general terms will be sufficient for our purposes. We can imagine the visionOntv of 2011/12 positioned on a diagram along with other historical examples of video activist groups, such as Cinema Action, the Amber Film Collective, its parent organization Undercurrents, and others discussed in Chapter 2, with the axes of this diagram relating to such things as video production, distribution, and exhibition; creating spaces for, and facilitating, audience engagement with the videos; and organizational and operational considerations (such as being non-commercial, engaging with local communities, being run by volunteers). These axes map out the space of actual positions extant and historical video activist groups take on the diagram ("individual singularities") and the potential positions ("universal singularities") such groups might occupy in the future, based on the various metrics of the different axes (DeLanda 2006b, 30, 2011, Appendix). For example, since a desired emergent property of the assemblages within this diagram includes effecting social change (whether indirectly through simply raising consciousness, or more directly by fostering the formation of communities of social change), the metric for an axis concerning audience engagement might measure such things as audience size or the activity of the audience members within the spaces provided for them.

While the visionOntv of 2016/17 had undergone significant changes, it can be argued that it was still situated within the same diagram, since it still retained the same main characteristics as in 2011/12, even though the degree to which it had manifested these had changed. For example, even though the focus of visionOntv's core team during the 2016/17 fieldwork was not directly focused on video distribution, the automated nature of the main components of the assemblage in its 2016/17 configuration, and its stability during that period of the fieldwork, meant that visionOntv continued to distribute videos. In addition, while visionOntv only produced two short activist videos during the 2016/17 fieldwork period, there were over 1,200 videos available on their YouTube account. So, while the fact that the audience for their videos had declined over the intervening years, which was no doubt exacerbated by the fact they were rarely making new videos (which were the only videos on their YouTube channel that they promoted on social media), they continued to attract an audience. And while visionOntv were no longer actively trying to facilitate discussions around the videos they distributed, they still maintained spaces within YouTube and Liferay for this, and the YouTube channel at least was still garnering comments. So, while the changes visionOntv underwent meant that it had changed its position along some of the diagrammatic axes meaning that it now occupied a different singularity, it was still describable by those same axes.

Of course, the precarious nature of the assemblage, due to its heavy dependence on YouTube, meant absolute deterritorialization threatened if visionOntv's account was closed, as this would signal a profound change in its identity. Similarly, while the OMN was still in the very early stages of its development, and the plans for it in 2016/17 meant that it could be considered in part as developing the video distribution aspect of visionOntv's assemblage (even though its scope was wider than that), how the OMN developed over time, and how visionOntv's 2016/17 assemblage integrated into it, remained to be seen and could also potentially change its identity such that it would no longer be described by the current diagram.

Conclusion

VisionOntv's core team's approach in 2011/12 to achieving their goal of promoting social change through the Internet using video was a broad one: We saw that they produced videos, trained others in video production, distributed their videos and those of others, and developed their own distribution platform as a model for others to adopt and use. To achieve this goal, the core members were engaged in many ongoing processes to construct and stabilize the visionOntv assemblage with respect to the wide variety of people and technologies that were a part of it. We saw, however, that some of these processes required a considerable amount of work as, for example, the interests of different actors were aligned with those of visionOntv, and the various destabilization processes were countered. As part of this, we saw that far from being pliable and dutiful components, the different technologies involved were actants in their own right, and visionOntv had to work to bring them into their assemblage and to keep them there.

This prominence of the theme of work within the ethnography was to be expected given Latour's observation of its centrality within the concept of actor-networks, as discussed in the first section, and we saw here that its demands were a limiting factor on visionOntv's agency. Sometimes it was the specialist nature of the work that resulted in restricting their agency, such as the situations where they were not able to make the technologies function the way they needed them to function (such as with the torrent technology, the RSS feed, and the Liferay upgrade), and sometimes it was simply the volume of the work required to maintain existing operations (such as the training of replacement volunteers, fixing relatively mundane technical problems, making Facebook and Twitter posts to maintain audiences, and supporting the nascent nodes of the macro assemblage), which drained their limited time and resources away from progressing their venture towards its goal. Paying attention to the impact the burden of work had on the agency of the visionOntv assemblage alerts us to the importance of funding, even in an Internet milieu where there is a large array of freely available video hosting, social media, and other kinds of platforms and technologies to draw upon: Insufficient funding meant that visionOntv was not able to employ specialist and other staff to take on some of this burden, which is of course common practice in better funded Internet ventures. This burden of work also contributed to the precarious nature of the assemblage, as visionOntv's core team and volunteers did not always have time to perform all the stabilizing processes that they believed were necessary, such as providing more support for the MSRN.

The precariousness of their assemblage was also due, amongst other reasons, to the asymmetrical power relations that existed between visionOntv and the organizations that provided them with the platforms they used. Ultimately, for example, there was little visionOntv could do if YouTube decided to reject their claims of fair use and take down a video, or even close their account, nor did it have the power to contest Facebook's increased commercialization of posts in its attention economy that resulted in a decrease of visionOntv's audience reach. Vision-Ontv were of course reluctant users of these platforms, driven to them because of their problems with, and the limitations of, their preferred options (torrents and Liferay) and because of the lack of alternatives, an insight which builds upon Fuchs's (2015, 229) observation discussed in Chapter 2 concerning the "soft and almost invisible form of coercion" certain commercial platforms exert because of their monopolization of online networking and other services.

The restricted agency of the visionOntv assemblage, and the deterritorialization processes it underwent in the intervening years due to, amongst other things, the conflicting and asymmetric power relationships that existed between its various components, led to changes in visionOntv's identity as they abandoned their goal of facilitating conversations and focused on developing a much more modest version of their macro assemblage concept. Overall, in spite of the fact that visionOntv were successful in producing and distributing a very large number of activist videos during the 2011/12 fieldwork period, and continued to do so into 2016/17, their ultimate objectives as video activists had not been achieved.

Notes

1 In this chapter, the term "visionOntv" when used without any qualification is a reference to it as an organization. Organizations in common parlance are attributed with beliefs and intentions, and this convention will be followed here, although of course the source and composition of these will be analysed throughout the chapter.
2 One "strike" is scored for each successful content removal request. With three strikes, the YouTube account is suspended and all videos are removed, and the user is prohibited from opening a new account (YouTube 2013).
3 This strategy also served the additional purpose of broadening visionOntv's audience base, which will be discussed in the next section.
4 More information on how this program works can be found at http://www.telestream.net/wirecast/overview.htm.
5 It should be noted that some configurations of the pop-up studio ran relatively trouble free, as they relied on fewer and simpler components, and because some of the components they used were already integrated together, such as a camera built into a laptop.
6 The territorialization and deterritorialization processes in this situation can alternatively be framed in terms of their roles in defining, stabilizing, and destabilizing *spatial* boundaries (DeLanda 2006b, 12–13), where space is interpreted here as online space rather than physical space: VisionOntv was trying to define the boundaries of the MSRN's online space, or at least define the proper space for its conversations, as being within the MSRN section

of the visionOntv platform, and resist the destabilization of this boundary which occurred with the inclusion of the Facebook group as an alternative online space for MSRN.

While DeLanda appears to reserve the spatial form of territorialization for "actual territories" and considers computer-based communications as contributing to deterritorialization since they "blur the spatial boundaries of social entities by eliminating the need for co-presence" (DeLanda 2006b, 13), extending the spatial aspect of territorialization as above seems appropriate given the general acceptance of the concept of "online spaces" both in academic and common parlance, particularly in situations, such as this one, where physical "co-presence" was neither the defining nor primary mode of interaction for most of those involved.

7 The scale of Facebook's resources is illustrated by the following metrics: Based on the most recent data available in the public domain at the time of writing, it had 18,770 employees (Facebook 2017a), owned an estimated $3.6 B of network equipment (including such things as server farms) (Data Center Knowledge 2016), and turned over $27.6 B (Facebook 2017b). While reliable, comparative, public domain data does not exist for Liferay, it had an estimated 550 employees at the end of 2014 (Rogers 2014).

8 Such a situation would be similar to that experienced by visionOntv with regard to the errant Blip RSS feed discussed in the first section.

References

Boland, Brian. 2014. *Organic Reach on Facebook: Your Questions Answered.* Facebook, [cited June 27 2017]. Available from www.facebook.com/business/news/Organic-Reach-on-Facebook.

Callon, Michel. 1980. "Struggles and Negotiations to Define What Is Problematic and What Is Not: The Socio-Logic of Translation." *The Social Process of Scientific Investigation* no. 4:197–219.

Callon, Michel. 1986. "Some Elements of a Sociology of Translation: The Domestication of the Scallops and St Brieuac Fishermen." In *Power, Action and Belief*, edited by J. Law, 196–232. London: Routledge and Kegan Paul.

Callon, Michel, and Bruno Latour. 1981. "Unscrewing the Big Leviathan: How Actors Macro-Structure Reality and How Sociologists Help Them to Do So." In *Advances in Social Theory and Methodology: Toward an Integration of Micro-and Macro-Sociologies*, edited by K. Knorr-Cetina and A.V. Cicourel, 277–303. Abingdon: Routledge.

Callon, Michel, and John Law. 1982. "On Interests and Their Transformation: Enrolment and Counter-Enrolment." *Social Studies of Science* no. 12 (4): 615–625.

Costanza-Chock, S. 2008. New Media Activism: Looking beyond the Last 5 Minutes. http://web.mit.edu/schock/www/docs/new_media_activism.pdf.

Data Center Knowledge. 2016. *The Facebook Data Center FAQ.* Data Center Knowledge, [cited July 4 2017]. Available from www.datacenterknowledge.com/the-facebook-data-center-faq-page-2/.

DeLanda, Manuel. 2006a. "Deleuzian Social Ontology and Assemblage Theory." In *Deleuze and the Social*, edited by M. Fuglsang and B.M. Sørensen, 250–266. Edinburgh: Edinburgh University Press.

DeLanda, Manuel. 2006b. *A New Philosophy of Society: Assemblage Theory and Social Complexity.* London: Continuum (Kindle Edition).

DeLanda, Manuel. 2010. *Deleuze: History and Science*. New York: Atropos.

DeLanda, Manuel. 2011. *Philosophy and Simulation: The Emergence of Synthetic Reason*. London: Continuum (Kindle Edition).

DeLanda, Manuel. 2016. *Assemblage Theory*. Edinburgh: Edinburgh University Press.

Deleuze, Gilles, and Claire Parnet. 2006. *Dialogues II*. London: Continuum.

Facebook. 2016. *How Do I Boost a Post from My Page?* Facebook, [cited December 12 2016]. Available from www.facebook.com/business/help/3478395 48598012?helpref=uf_permalink.

Facebook. 2017a. *Company Info*. Facebook, [cited July 4 2017]. Available from https://newsroom.fb.com/company-info/.

Facebook. 2017b. *Facebook Reports Fourth Quarter and Full Year 2016 Results*. Facebook, [cited July 4 2017]. Available from https://investor.fb.com/investor-news/press-release-details/2017/facebook-Reports-Fourth-Quarter-and-Full-Year-2016-Results/default.aspx.

Fenton, N. 2012. "The Internet and Social Networking." In *Misunderstanding the Internet*, edited by J. Curran, N. Fenton, and D. Freedman, 123–148. Abingdon: Routledge.

Fuchs, Christian. 2015. *Culture and Economy in the Age of Social Media*. New York: Routledge.

Gane, Nicholas. 2004. *The Future of Social Theory*. London: Continuum.

Hess, Aaron. 2009. "Resistance Up in Smoke: Analyzing the Limitations of Deliberation on YouTube." *Critical Studies in Media Communication* no. 26 (5):411–434. doi:10.1080/15295030903325347.

Juhasz, Alexandra. 2008. "Documentary on YouTube: The Failure of the Direct Cinema of the Slogan." In *Re-Thinking Documentary*, edited by Thomas Austin. New York: McGraw Hill.

Lange, Patricia G. 2017. "Participatory Complications in Interactive, Video-Sharing Environments." In *The Routledge Companion to Digital Ethnography*, edited by Larissa Hjorth, Heather Horst, Anne Galloway, and Genevieve Bell, 147–157. New York: Routledge.

Latour, Bruno. 1987. *Science in Action: How to Follow Scientists and Engineers through Society*. Cambridge, MA: Harvard University Press.

Latour, Bruno. 1999. *Pandora's Hope: Essays on the Reality of Science Studies*. Cambridge, MA: Harvard University Press.

Latour, Bruno. 2005. *Reassembling the Social*. Oxford: Oxford University Press.

Law, John. 1992. "Notes on the Theory of the Actor-Network: Ordering, Strategy, and Heterogeneity." *Systemic Practice and Action Research* no. 5 (4):379–393.

Law, John. 2003. Traduction/Trahison: Notes on ANT. www.lancaster.ac.uk/sociology/research/publications/papers/law-traduction-trahison.pdf.

Law, John. 2009. "Actor Network Theory and Material Semiotics." In *The New Blackwell Companion to Social Theory*, edited by B. Turner, 141–158. Oxford: Wiley-Blackwell.

Law, John, and Annemarie Mol. 2008. "The Actor-Enacted: Cumbrian Sheep in 2001." In *Material Agency: Towards a Non-anthropocentric Approach*, edited by Carl Knappett and Lambros Malafouris, 57–77. New York: Springer.

Presence, Steve. 2015. "The Contemporary Landscape of Video-Activism in Britain." In *Marxism and Film Activism: Screening Alternative Worlds*, edited by Ewa Mazierska and Lars Kristensen, 186–212. Oxford: Berghahn Books.

Rivera, Gibran, and Andrew M. Cox. 2016. "An Actor-Network Theory Perspective to Study the Non-Adoption of a Collaborative Technology Intended to Support Online Community Participation." *Academia Revista Latinoamericana de Administración* no. 29 (3):347–365.

Rogers, Bruce. 2014. *Bryan Cheung's Liferay Is Doing Well To Do Well.* Forbes, [cited July 4 2017]. Available from www.forbes.com/sites/brucerogers/2014/10/31/bryan-cheungs-liferay-is-doing-well-to-do-well/-52d469b726d8.

Salovaara, Inka. 2015. "Media Spaces of Fluid Politics Participatory Assemblages and Networked Narratives." *Media Transformations* no. 11:10–29.

visionOntv. 2011. *Making News Roadshow in Liverpool.* Facebook, [cited April 5 2013]. Available from www.facebook.com/events/132869300120675/.

visionOntv. 2013. *Produce.* visionOntv, [cited July 22 2013]. Available from http://visionon.tv/produce.

YouTube. 2013. *Copyright Strike Basics.* YouTube, [cited March 27 2013]. Available from http://support.google.com/youtube/bin/answer.py?hl=en&answer=2814000.

5 The LiveJournal Vidding Community

Fan Video Makers

This chapter, following the approach of the previous one, analyses the complex arrangements of people, machines, and other components the LiveJournal vidding community used to distribute their film and television fan videos, showing how these arrangements can be understood in terms of the theoretical concepts of Assemblage Theory and ANT. We saw in Chapter 2 that these videos were typically montages of scenes from films and television series reworked and set to music. The community's purpose for doing this was typically to explore different themes within the source material and to share this exploration with others. Specifically, some community members used video making as a way of highlighting aspects of the source material, particularly related to things that were not obvious, such as subtexts and aspects relating to secondary characters; others saw fan video making as a way to respond to the source material, as a way of "talking back" to it, or even as a way of subverting it; still others saw it as a method to construct arguments about a show and as the preferred medium for doing this over fan fiction and fan art.[1]

The first section of this chapter, based on the 2011/12 fieldwork, examines the primarily human and machine components that made up the assemblages constructed to distribute these videos. It begins with an analysis of LiveJournal, the journaling platform that was central to the community's activities during this period, and includes a detailed investigation of how the community's members interacted with each other through it, and then moves to a discussion of the video hosting platforms and other components used by the community. The section's focus is on analysing the various processes these components and the assemblages that included them underwent as part of the community's distribution activities and shows that the community members were struggling against processes that threatened to destabilize their assemblages. The second section, based on the 2016/17 fieldwork, explores how the community had undergone significant changes since 2011/12 due to the ongoing destabilization processes that they faced, and examines the counter-processes that the community employed in an attempt to stabilize its identity.

The Distribution Assemblages and Their Components: Construction, Stabilization, and Destabilization

As stated in Chapter 2, the LiveJournal vidding community had its roots in the earliest days of fan video making, many years before the advent of the Internet as a video distribution technology. We also saw in Chapter 2 that the components of their pre-Internet distribution assemblage consisted of fan videos copied to physical media that circulated through their community and of geographically dispersed video makers and their audiences that made up that community. Other components included venues where the community was temporarily spatially "territorialized" (DeLanda 2006b, 13), such as fan convention spaces and private residences, where distribution and exhibition primarily took place, and various elements of the postal service that sent videos between community members.

To understand how and why their assemblage took the form it did when I first encountered it in 2011, it is necessary to understand the circumstances surrounding the community's adoption of the Internet before this time, which occurred in two distinct phases. The first phase involved the use of the Internet for various fan-related activities prior to its adoption for video distribution. These activities included text-based discussions about fan videos and about different film and television programmes, as well as the sharing of fan fiction and images. The community had in fact fairly rapidly integrated the Internet into their activities, with some members having used various technologies such as email lists and bulletin boards since the mid-1990s to engage with each other. One of the main platforms used was the Yahoo Groups "vidder" email list, whose purpose was to provide a place for video makers and their audiences to discuss the various aspects of fan video making and viewing.

Journaling platforms and the transition to Internet video distribution. The community began to adopt LiveJournal in the early 2000s, which eventually supplanted the email lists and bulletin boards as its primary communication platform.[2] This adoption took the form of a series of "translation" processes (Callon 1980, 211; Latour 2005, 108) that both reconfigured the community's assemblage and also helped to stabilize it. For example, unlike email lists and bulletin boards, Live-Journal created a private space for each user. This was during a period of the Internet when creating and maintaining one's own personal web site would have required some technical knowledge and not insignificant cost. While community members often felt constrained by email lists, believing that long posts or posting too often was poor etiquette as it could potentially overwhelm list members with too much information, the private nature of the LiveJournal page meant that users felt free to discuss their thoughts on fan videos more often and at greater length, in the knowledge that only those interested in visiting their page would come across them. Because LiveJournal also included a threaded comments feature – allowing users to both comment on a journal post and also to comment on those comments – posts could generate ongoing conversations involving several community members, which were available for others to read.

These LiveJournal posts and comments can be analysed as actants that interested some community members enough to leave their own comments, and their process of doing so was a translation since, following one of Latour's (2005, 108) formulations, it allowed the commenter's LiveJournal account to coexist with the original poster's account by connecting them together: These comments automatically included links to the commenters' LiveJournal accounts within them and also automatically created a message in the original poster's LiveJournal inbox that also included a link to the commenter's account. In addition to the connections these actants made between the technological components of the assemblage, they also connected the human components through the conversations that developed since, using one of Callon's (1980, 211) framings of translation, they often resulted in a convergence and expressions of shared ideas and understandings (although sometimes they did the opposite, which is discussed below). Since having a LiveJournal account was required before one could leave a comment, such posts were also actants that enrolled community members into LiveJournal. These posts and comments also acted to stabilize the enrolment of LiveJournal in the community, as they encouraged members to keep their accounts open so they could remain part of the ongoing conversations. With community members feeling less constrained in their use of LiveJournal versus the older Internet technologies, the number and depth of conversations also increased considerably, which in turn increased the community members' investment in LiveJournal, further stabilizing its enrolment within the community. Also, similar to DeLanda's (2016, 10–11) observations concerning the emergent property of density that can arise in interpersonal networks, the increasing number of connections between different community members brought about by these translation processes had a stabilizing effect on the community assemblage as a whole.

Other features of LiveJournal also helped stabilize the community's assemblage, such as the "friends list", which allowed users to add other users to a list, and these other users had the option to reciprocate or not. One of the key aspects of the friends list was that it could be used to restrict the circulation of journal posts: Journal posts were typically readable by anyone coming across the user's journal account, but LiveJournal gave the user the option of restricting their posts so that only those on their friends list were able to view them. Using the friends list option on posts was therefore a homogenization process of the kind DeLanda describes (2006b, 13), restricting them to only a certain category of user, excluding both users from outside the community and also those from within the community that were not on the list. This helped to stabilize the community's assemblage in different ways. One such way was to allow the user to post comments that might be interpreted as controversial by some members of the wider community, which could potentially lead to conflict within the community and destabilize it. Another way this feature helped stabilize the community was that it allowed the user to share intimate thoughts about fan-related or personal subjects with only the members of the community they thought would receive them sympathetically, which over time sometimes led to the strengthening of the bonds between the users involved. Another feature of the friends list related to an algorithm within LiveJournal that aggregated all the posts made by those on a user's friends list into a separate feed for the user to read. This meant that a user would only have to check their feed to stay up to date on their friends' activities, rather than having to visit every account separately, which helped to maintain the connections between different users, and therefore further stabilized the community's assemblage.

In addition to the private journal pages discussed above, LiveJournal also permitted the creation of shared, public journal pages. This functionality allowed for topic-specific LiveJournal webpages to be set up by users, and examples included "vividcon" and "vidukon", which were for discussions relating to those two fan video conventions, and "vidding", which was for discussions of fan videos. The user who set up the page acted as an administrator, and they could grant other users access to it, allowing them to make posts. The creation of these pages was a territorialization process that sought to homogenize discussion around topics important to the community in general, unlike the thematically heterogeneous discussions on the private journal pages, and provided shared spaces where the community as a whole could perform, contest, and stabilize the different aspects of its identity.

Using DeLanda's (2006a, 251–252) conceptualization of the relative scales of assemblages, the topology of LiveJournal outlined above for the fan community can be analysed as a macro assemblage of private and public pages. These pages were themselves micro assemblages, including components such as journal posts, comments, and a variety of other elements such as profile images, tags, and likes. The users of these pages were also components, whose enrolment was maintained within the micro assemblages by their interest in engaging with the posts, comments, and other digital artefacts created on these pages by other users and by LiveJournal's algorithmic and other technical actants. These actants included not only friends lists and feeds, but also other functionality such as "memories", which allowed other users' journal entries to be bookmarked for viewing again at a later date, and account dashboards that aggregated and allowed easy access to all the comments made by a user and all the comments received on their entries by other users. Finally, the work done by users, and by the algorithmic and other technical actants, also maintained the pages' enrolment within each other, meaning the community's LiveJournal macro assemblage was a web of densely interconnected pages. This LiveJournal macro assemblage was also itself a micro assemblage, functioning as the primary "expressive component" (DeLanda 2006b, 12) within the community's overall macro assemblage, which also included the components of the video distribution assemblage discussed above (for example, videotapes), as well as the older Internet technologies such as email lists that continued to operate alongside LiveJournal, although in a much-diminished capacity.

The second phase of the community's adoption of the Internet related to its use to distribute fan videos and took place after LiveJournal had become the primary platform for the community's day-to-day discursive activities. There was in fact intense debate within the community as to whether, and how, the Internet should be used for video distribution. Prior to the advent of the Internet, the community had circulated their work in strict confidence within their membership, avoiding the attention of outsiders for fear of being targeted by copyright holders of the source material and also because of concerns their work might be misunderstood or mocked by audiences unfamiliar with the poetics of their video making tradition, which we saw in Chapter 2 were concerns shared by other fan video makers also. These very restricted distribution practices were, amongst other things, territorialization processes that ensured the homogeneity of the audience with respect to attitudes towards copyright and fan video poetics.

Their dilemma was balancing, on the one hand, their desire to maintain the homogeneity of their assemblage, and avoid the potential destabilization enrolling Internet audiences into it might bring, while, on the other, taking advantage of the possibilities of Internet technologies for video distribution and also taking their place alongside other fan video groups on the Internet, echoing the concerns expressed in Chapter 2 that this kind of video making tradition might lose its place in history as other fan video forms proliferated on the Internet. To resolve this dilemma, some translated the Internet distribution technologies in ways that while limiting their utility, allowed them to coexist with the community's assemblage without destabilizing it. For example, some producers maintained their own websites, and anyone interested in viewing the videos they contained had to email the producer first requesting a password, which would then allow the would-be viewer to download the video file to their own computer. Passwords were, however, typically only granted to people known to the producer as a way of limiting a video's reach.

While some video makers in the community used this limited form of distribution, it took until 2007 before the use of the Internet to distribute videos became widespread in the community. The catalyst for it was a particular moment of translation. Laura, a community member, described it as follows:

> After attending a planning meeting for the DIY Video Summit in early 2007 and hearing the positive responses from the other makers

there, I posted to my [LiveJournal account] about it and came home to find that my corner of fandom had listened: Hundreds of vidders were putting their vids up for streaming at iMeem, and I did the same. It just took a little understanding of the milieu in which we were now operating – a much more open Internet in which home-made videos were commonplace – for most of my community to open its doors and begin offering our work online and unrestricted.

Analysing this event as a translation, we see that Laura acted as a "mediator" (Latour 2005, 39) between her community and elements of the wider Internet video culture. She enrolled LiveJournal as an actant in this process, and her post, another actant, made its way through the interconnected LiveJournal accounts of the different community members. Following Latour (1987, 117) and Callon (1980, 211), we see that Laura's post channelled her community in a different direction by offering a new interpretation of the Internet based on her experience at the planning meeting by relating things – her community and the wider Internet video culture – that were previously perceived as different. Laura's ability to rapidly mobilize her community through a single journal entry was due to the community assemblage's emergent property of density, mentioned above. For DeLanda (2016, 76), this is an intensive property, meaning that variations in quantitative aspects of an assemblage can cause it to undergo qualitative changes, and in the case of interpersonal networks, sufficiently dense networks have the qualitative property of being able to rapidly transmit relevant information through them, which was the case with Laura's journal entry. Also, LiveJournal, which was a critical actant in this communication, performed as an "intermediary" (Latour 2005, 39), transporting Laura's entry throughout the community network with fidelity.

There were several reasons for the eventual adoption of the Internet by the community's producers to distribute their videos, and these varied for different producers. Most of them had decided, once their fears were overcome, that distributing their videos via the Internet offered an opportunity for them to integrate their video distribution practices into their discursive practices on LiveJournal concerning those videos, which was not possible using physical media such as videocassette tapes and DVDs, and that this was a better way of engaging with their existing audience within the community. This was a homogenization process that acted on the producer's micro assemblages by introducing technologies that were better able to "co-function" (Deleuze and Parnet 2006, 52) with LiveJournal, and excluding those that were not, which, as we would expect from an Assemblage Theory perspective, gave rise to emergent properties that helped stabilize the community's assemblages as we shall see below.

Also, some producers saw the community as only a small part of their target audience, with Internet distribution technologies providing a way to reach people who would never consider going to a fan convention or requesting physical media to be sent to them. Finally, though, there were some producers who adopted these technologies who would rather have continued using physical media than the Internet and who were also not interested in reaching an audience beyond the community. "Georgia" (a pseudonym), for example, still held onto the concerns (during the period of the 2011/12 fieldwork) about Internet distribution discussed above, believing that people who did not know the source material very well could easily misunderstand her videos. For her, fan videos were a form of community dialogue that took place at VividCon and with "fannish" friends. She in fact appreciated the relatively cumbersome nature of physical media distribution, believing that videotape cassettes and DVDs would be unlikely to spread very far beyond the recipients to whom she supplied them. But she acknowledged that the community's expectations were such that videos had to be available online for anyone to be interested in viewing them, and therefore she had adopted these technologies as a stabilization process to maintain her audience.

Integrating Internet video distribution technologies with LiveJournal involved a translation: Since it did not support video hosting at the time, the producers hosted their videos elsewhere, and used certain features of both the hosting platforms and LiveJournal to include videos in their LiveJournal posts. While the elements of this translation relating directly to the hosting platforms will be discussed in detail below, LiveJournal's part in it involved a producer posting a journal entry announcing a new video, which included a note on the visual source material and music used, a summary of the video's contents, plus some other information including LiveJournal search tags. It also, most importantly, included a video embedded within an html frame in the journal entry and hypertext links pointing to downloadable versions of the video, created by using LiveJournal functionality. Comments by the audience about the video were appended at the bottom of the journal entry. This translation involved making the LiveJournal entry and the video converge by using functionality within LiveJournal to transform the video into something that could coexist with the entry.

Although LiveJournal had become the central component in the community's video distribution assemblage by the time I encountered it in 2011, its enrolment had begun to destabilize as some community members became dissatisfied with it, which had caused them to explore alternatives. The first signs of this dissatisfaction emerged during an event that was referred to as "Strikethrough" within the community, which occurred in mid-2007. This event involved LiveJournal's platform administrators deleting some journals, the names of which after deletion appeared in strikethrough font in the friends lists of other users that had previously added them. LiveJournal's explanation for this was that they were removing journals that listed such things as child pornography, incest, paedophilia, and rape in their keywords, since journals of this kind were not welcome on the platform, but they accepted that innocent journals, such as those of rape survivor groups or fan groups, had also inadvertently been deleted (Fanlore 2017). The vidding community suspected other motives however, primarily that LiveJournal's owners were removing controversial content to make the platform more advertiser-friendly, and therefore some believed that the deletion of fan journals was not an accident.

The Strikethrough controversy caused some of the vidding community's members to question their use of the platform. For example, because some of the culled journals related to homosexuality, slash video makers feared that they might eventually be censored by the platform. Others felt betrayed by LiveJournal, as there was a feeling by some in the community that the financial and other support of fan communities in the early days of the platform's existence had helped it to establish itself. Also, further undermining the community's commitment to the platform was the belief amongst some members that there had been a distinctive change in the attitude of LiveJournal's staff towards the platform's users following the Strikethrough controversy: Some community members believed it had gone from an organization that worked collaboratively with users to develop a platform that met their needs to one that seemed primarily motived by financial return regardless of the implications for its users. Finally, the actual technical instability of the platform itself was also contributing to the destabilization of LiveJournal's enrolment within the community. The causes of this instability were periodic denial-of-service attacks, which some community members suspected related to the prominence of LiveJournal amongst Russian political dissidents, and these attacks had become sufficiently disruptive to contribute to some members' desire for an alternative platform.

These various destabilizing processes show, therefore, that LiveJournal did not always simply behave as an intermediary, as in the case of its dutiful propagation of Laura's post discussed earlier, but sometimes it also behaved as a mediator in the ANT sense, where its specificity as an actor had to be taken into account. In the situations described above, it was an assemblage of people and machines (amongst other things) that on the one hand occasionally underwent territorialization processes to homogenize its components (journals, the people involved in its development) so as to achieve results that sometimes diverged from those of the vidder community. On the other hand, it was an assemblage that sometimes underwent "deterritorialization" processes (DeLanda 2006b, 12) caused by third-party actors (denial-of-service attacks). In both cases, these processes destabilized LiveJournal's enrolment within the community's assemblages.

In response to this destabilization of LiveJournal, some community members began including an additional platform within their micro assemblages, Dreamwidth, which was at the time a relatively new journaling website. It was perceived within the community as a "fannish" social media platform, coded with fans in mind, and developed by people who came from fandom and who were responsive to input from the community concerning its development. This inclusion of Dreamwidth was therefore a territorialization process as it increased the homogeneity of the members' micro assemblages by placing the "fannish" Dreamwidth at their centre in place of LiveJournal. However, its inclusion was also potentially a deterritorialization process for the community's macro assemblage, as it threatened to destabilize it by increasing its heterogeneity through the introduction of another journaling platform and risked splitting the community into two separate groups. Dreamwidth, however, included a cross-posting function that could be used to simultaneous post entries to LiveJournal: This function was an actant employed by those who had moved to Dreamwidth to maintain LiveJournal's enrolment within their micro assemblages, and thereby their enrolment within the community's macro assemblage, stabilizing the macro assemblage with very little additional work.

The community's video producers engaged in sustained online interactions with their audiences about their videos, and the primary public form these took were text discussions on the journaling sites, typically occurring in the comments section below the producer's journal entry announcing the video. These online interactions were generally considered to be a very important aspect of the community's activities and were highly valued by the producers. They involved direct feedback from other community members on the videos, as well as responses from the producer to this feedback, in addition to exchanges between the audience members themselves, although this last type of interaction was less common. Topics included various aspects of the videos, including editing techniques, song choice, and themes, as well as more general discussions concerning fan video making and the fandoms addressed in the videos. While producers welcomed short, celebratory comments, more detailed discussions were typically seen as at least as important.

The following example of the more detailed kind of discussion concerns a video posted by Obsessive24 on her LiveJournal account, which explores the unrequited love of Riley for Buffy, characters from the series *Buffy the Vampire Slayer*.[3] There were over 40 comments made on the video during a six-month period from the date of the original journal post. The first was a long comment by Speranza, at over 150 words long. The comment had two main themes. First, it was a celebration of the video because it agreed with Speranza's reading of the Buffy/Riley relationship, and second, it provided her analysis of why the *Buffy* television audience did not take to Riley as a character. Another community member, here's luck, made a very short comment on this comment supporting it, and Obsessive24 also replied to Speranza's comment thanking her for it and then giving her own thoughts on the audience reception of Riley. The remaining comments and replies varied considerably in length. Some were very short, celebratory comments, which typically received very short but polite responses from Obsessive24. Some, however, were very detailed: One comment was 900 words long and contained an analysis of the video using time codes. Obsessive24's response was also long, running to nearly 300 words.

These comments were actants that helped stabilize the community by creating or renewing the connections between, primarily, producers and their audiences within the community. Drawing upon Law's formulation of actants, the comments can be conceptualized as the "continuously generated effect of the webs of relations within which they [were] located" (2009, 141): The journal entries announcing the videos were actants that interested some community members into viewing the videos (for example, because of an interest in the source, theme, or song choice mentioned in the entry), and the videos themselves were actants that in turn sufficiently interested some of these viewers into leaving a comment. Also, the journals more generally were actants enrolled into this translation process since their discursive nature and ubiquity in the community both encouraged commenting and reduced the work of doing so. As this example illustrates, and which was common practice, the producers engaged in work to encourage these comments by responding to the comments left, with most producers responding to every comment, if only to express gratitude. Beyond this, they were also meant as positive reinforcement to reassure commenters who might have been hesitant to leave a comment so as to encourage them to leave comments in the future.

Comments on video journal entries were often only the first part of the process of establishing and maintaining the connections between producers and their audiences within the community: After the initial exchange of comments, and when the producer and audience member shared sufficient interest in doing so, the discussion would move to other, more private, online and offline spaces, developing over time in different directions, sometimes eventually involving the sharing of intimate details concerning their lives, and in some cases forming into close friendships. These spaces included a dedicated fan video chat room on IRC, private instant messaging services, Skype, telephone, and face to face meetings at conventions and privately. Moving discussions from the relatively public space of journals to more private spaces was in fact a stabilization process: Not only did this facilitate more personal and intimate exchanges, thereby potentially allowing for the formation of more substantial connections, but it also allowed for the private discussions of issues related to videos that might be considered controversial by some members of the community.

Video critiques were one type of potentially controversial discussion: Conflicts had previously arisen in the community when critiques done in public had been interpreted by the producer or third-party community members negatively. These destabilized the community by threating to rupture the connections between the members caught up in the conflict, which could potentially lead to some community members' micro assemblages becoming detached from the macro assemblage or lead to the breaking up of the community into smaller groups that no longer interacted with each other. Concerns about precipitating such conflicts had resulted in community members avoiding giving constructive criticism in public in recent years, as well as avoiding other kinds of comments that might be considered controversial. While this increased "coding" (DeLanda 2010, 13) of the community's use of language in public helped to stabilize it, some members lamented the resulting loss of critical comment caused by the restrictions the emergence of this new, implicit norm put on the community's communicative practices.

The roles of the video hosting platforms and other components. Like LiveJournal, Dreamwidth was unable to host videos, and so the community's producers hosted them elsewhere and embedded them in journal entries in a similar fashion to that described above for LiveJournal. Decisions concerning which particular hosting platforms to use, and how to use them, rested heavily on the likely stability of the resulting assemblage. Unsurprisingly, stability issues relating to copyright featured prominently in the community's decision calculus. Some producers choose relatively low-profile hosting platforms, such as Viddler, in the belief that their videos were much less likely to come to the attention of copyright holders, and therefore running a lower risk of having their videos taken down or having their hosting accounts closed.

Copyright considerations also meant that many producers avoided using YouTube: There was a general feeling of hostility towards YouTube within the community, as it was perceived as an organization with a history of enforcing spurious copyright claims, prone to arbitrary and unexplained takedowns of videos, and with an uncharitable interpretation of fair use (a concept that was introduced in Chapter 2). This led to an "anything but YouTube" mentality for many of the producers, which was an acknowledgement by them that it would be difficult to maintain YouTube's enrolment within their assemblages for the long term because of their divergent interests related to copyright and fair use and that they had relatively little power to translate YouTube's interests into something that was compatible with their own.

Some producers, however, wanted their videos to reach a larger audience than either their journals or the less prominent hosting services could reach, and so they reluctantly decided to embrace YouTube. These producers, however, received regular Digital Millennium Copyright Act (DMCA) notices from YouTube that claimed copyright infringement on videos that the producers considered covered by the Act's fair use provisions.[4] To prevent their videos from being taken down, and to avoid receiving a "strike" on their YouTube accounts (a punitive action discussed in Chapter 4), producers were required to respond to these notices and assert their claim of fair use. Responding to these notices was an ongoing process of translation to prevent destabilization of YouTube's enrolment in the producers' assemblages: Drawing upon Callon's (1986, 207) formulation of translations as an alignment of interests, the producers were required to repeatedly work to reaffirm to YouTube that their interests where in fact aligned with respect to the hosted videos' legal compliance (a discussion of this translation process with respect to YouTube, and of the conflicts that arose between it and the producers related to their divergent interests, will be deferred until the next section where it will be analysed in detail).

These difficulties the community had with YouTube arose from the fact that it was an assemblage in its own right attempting to stabilize itself: YouTube had come under legal threat in the years preceding the fieldwork from copyright holders of music, film, and television properties who saw it as undermining their businesses (see, for example, *Viacom Int'l, Inc. v. YouTube, Inc.*, No. 07-CV-02103 (S.D.N.Y. 2007)). The serving of DMCA notices was a territorialization process whose purpose was to homogenize the content they hosted so that it was copyright compliant, in an attempt to stave off these legal challenges. These notices, as well as having what can be understood as a "material role" in the computational processes that sometimes led to a video being taken down and strikes being allocated to accounts, also had an "expressive role" (DeLanda 2006b, 12) in that they were written documents. They were also actants that in turn enacted YouTube's terms of service statement, another written document performing an expressive role in YouTube's assemblage.[5] These two types of written documents encouraged copyright compliance and threatened sanctions if such compliance was not forthcoming and, therefore, can be understood as part of a coding stabilization process.

The fact that the DMCA notice process threatened to destabilize the producers' micro assemblages that included YouTube, even though these producers believed that they were compliant with both YouTube's terms of service and with the fair use provisions within copyright law, was a result of insufficient coding: Although the concept of fair use was described by copyright law, and by YouTube's terms of service, there was enough ambiguity in the concept when applied to fan videos to allow YouTube, copyright holders, and the community's producers to interpret it in different ways. This ambiguity was due to the absence of case law at the time relating to fan video and fair use: These judgments, had they existed, would have been included as additional components in the assemblages, whose expressive role would have been to reduce the possible legal interpretations concerning fair use, thereby using language to further code and stabilize the producers' assemblages (assuming the producers' videos were complaint with the judgements).

While YouTube's attitude to fair use was generally reviled by the community, some producers appreciated the fact that at least YouTube provided a process for them to challenge copyright claims, unlike some hosting platforms that simply took videos down without notice or recourse for the user, offering them an opportunity to stabilize their assemblages in the face of a considerable power asymmetry, even though it generated work for them and risked failure. In spite of the existence of this stabilization process, many producers remained concerned both by YouTube's attitude with respect to fair use and by the fact that its very high profile was more likely to attract the attention of copyright holders, and so they continued to avoid it during the period of the 2011/12 fieldwork.

Others, however, took a middle path concerning YouTube and used it in a restricted way. For example, one producer maintained a YouTube account only for a small number of videos that she believed appealed to a general YouTube audience, but used a different pseudonym for this account than the one she used for the main part of her distribution assemblage to avoid her other work being connected to any copyright issues arising on YouTube. This enabled her to use YouTube to attract a larger audience for those videos than would have been possible using the main part of her distribution assemblage, while also protecting the stability of that part of her assemblage by keeping it separated from YouTube. Restricting the use of hosting platforms because of copyright concerns was also a stabilization process employed by some producers using hosting platforms other than YouTube. For example, users of Vimeo typically password protected their videos to limit their potential audience to only those people who found their videos through their journals: The password was typically provided just below the video embedded within the journal entry announcing it and was not available otherwise.

Producers' decisions concerning which particular hosting platforms to use, and their evaluations of how the different alternatives would affect the stability of the resulting assemblages, took into account factors in addition to those relating to copyright. One such factor was the producers' assessment of the stability of the video hosting platforms themselves, which were assemblages in their own right, and sometime precarious ones, as noted above. This was a serious concern for the community dating back to their experiences with iMeem, which, as we saw, was the first hosting platform they had adopted en masse.[6] Around two years after their initial adoption of it, iMeem announced that it would no longer host videos and only gave its users a few days' notice of their intentions. Not long after this announcement, iMeem in fact went permanently offline, and it was speculated that this was due to financial difficulties. The community producers' enrolment of iMeem within their respective micro assemblages failed as a result, and they were powerless to prevent this from happening. This caused the community considerable disruption because alternative hosting had to be sought, all their videos had to be uploaded again, and journal entries containing embeds and links had to be updated. Also comments on videos, hit counts, and even some videos that were not backed up were lost.

Failure of key functionality within the hosting platforms was also another source of instability for the community members' assemblages. For example, Laura used Blip to host her videos but discovered one day that the videos she had embedded from there into her LiveJournal pages were no longer working, even though they were still available directly from Blip. This situation went on for some time, and Laura believed that Blip did not have sufficient resources to deal with problems like these in a timely fashion. In fact, the developing perception in the community during the 2011/12 fieldwork was that the economic viability, and hence the reliability, of the hosting platforms other than YouTube was questionable.

Overall, the enrolments of all the third-party video hosting platforms were precarious, which contributed to the precariousness of the community's assemblages. These enrolments were precarious because either the platforms themselves were precarious assemblages or because the translations upon which the enrolments depended lacked fidelity (in Law's (2003) sense of this term), as they relied upon the insufficiently defined concept of fair use that was sometimes interpreted differently by the different actors involved. These different interpretations primarily emerged out of the divergent interests of the actors involved with respect to copyright, undermining the translations of the hosting platforms, which, given the power asymmetry between the producers and the platforms, proved difficult to stabilize. While each producer weighed up the different types of risks and benefits associated with each platform relative to their own objectives as fan video makers, many were forced to make compromises that they were unhappy with. For example, after her experience with Blip, Laura had very reluctantly decided to use YouTube, as she was concerned about the long-term viability of the smaller platforms.

Since there were few options available to stabilize the enrolments of the individual hosting platforms, producers uploaded their videos to more than one platform to provide redundancy, thereby reducing the precariousness of their assemblages' overall hosting arrangements. While this strategy typically involved using two or more third-party platforms, some community members also maintained their own websites alongside these platforms. These websites did not stream the videos, but simply made them available for downloading, providing a backup copy, and the links to these were provided in the journal posts announcing the videos as mentioned above.[7]

While redundant hosting and redundant journaling (provided by using Dreamwidth alongside LiveJournal, as discussed previously) meant that the community's assemblages were relatively stable around the time of the 2011/12 fieldwork, there was a strong desire within the community for a permanent repository for their videos and associated elements such as view counts, comments, and likes. This desire had led some producers to use the Archive of Our Own (AO3) platform. This was a platform developed and run by the Organization of Transformative Works (OTW), a non-profit fan-run organization, and built on the open source "Ruby on Rails" web development framework (Archive of Our Own 2013). It was initially designed as a platform for fan fiction, and although it was not able to host videos, it did allow producers to create a directory of their videos and embed and tag them there, and it also tracked video view counts and allowed for comments to be left under the embedded videos by others with AO3 accounts. While this functionality was sufficient to interest some producers in using it, others felt that without video hosting functionality, they couldn't justify the extra work involved in creating entries for all their existing and new videos on an additional platform.

The reason the OTW had delayed including video hosting within AO3 was that they had yet to find a way of doing this that would result in AO3 remaining stable. For example, the OTW had avoided developing a conventional video streaming service as the risk was that, given their popular subject matter, some videos could "go viral" and this would overload OTW's servers and consume excessive bandwidth, threatening the stability of both AO3 and the OTW itself. The OTW had considered using torrent technology as an alternative to streaming since this overcame server and bandwidth constraints by distributing hosting through client computers, but this was a problematic solution also: The perception within OTW was that Internet service providers throttled torrent bandwidths because of concerns over their legality, and therefore the resulting quality of the viewing experience would not be high enough to interest users. Since neither conventional streaming solutions nor torrent solutions were satisfactory for their needs, the OTW was delaying making a decision, waiting for open source developers to provide alternative solutions that they might be able to adapt for their purposes. Developing a video hosting solution was therefore a complex translation process for the OTW, requiring them to align the interests of various human, technological, and organizational actors, and this process was still ongoing by the end of the fieldwork in 2012.

In addition to the journals, hosting platforms, and AO3, producers also used other online technologies to distribute their videos. Some, for example, had begun to experiment with Tumblr. Like the journaling sites, Tumblr did not host videos, but enabled them to be embedded within posts to the site. Tumblr was seen as a way of reaching a different audience from the journals, having a younger audience and one more interested in the immediate impact of shared images than in lengthy text discussions. It was also believed that particular fandoms, such as that of the television series *Glee*, were focused on Tumblr.

Some producers also used Facebook and Twitter, although this was not common, as almost all of the community kept their fan activities separate from activities in their legal names, and at the time, it was generally considered superfluous to maintain pseudonymous social media accounts in addition to the journals. Those who used them did so to announce their new videos to people who were part of their wider social network but who did not follow their journals. They did this by making a post that contained a short text comment about the video and a link to the entry announcing the video on LiveJournal or Dreamwidth. These posts were actants that performed translations by using the text comment to interest the reader in the video, persuading them to click on the associated link rather than read the next post or tweet in their social media feeds: Using one of Latour's (1987, 117) formulations of the concept of translation, these actants can be understood as "offering new interpretations of … interests and channelling people in different directions".

While the Internet-based components discussed above had largely displaced the traditional ones in the community's distribution assemblages by the time I encountered them in 2011, some remained. Primary amongst these were the fan video conventions, and VividCon in particular. One important role VividCon continued to have was as an actant that helped stabilize the community. Following Law's (2003, 3) observation that "links and nodes in the network do not last all by themselves but instead need constant maintenance work, the support of other links and nodes", VividCon was a "node" (actant), within the community's macro assemblage that helped stabilize the "links" (translations) between the other components of the macro assemblage. VividCon performed this role by providing an offline space where the community could reaffirm its shared values in ways that were not possible online, reinforcing the online stabilization processes, such as the interactions on the journals' video posts. The video premieres session during the convention, where producers would show their newly created videos to the community for the first time, was a prime example of this. These sessions would often evoke strong positive emotions in their attendees, typically numbering more than 100 community members gathered in the same screening room, who exhibited these through tears, waves of laughter, or enthusiastic applause, which were seen by many in the community as expressions of their shared values that helped to maintain the community's identity. The importance of the premieres session for the community was such that some producers held off uploading their newest videos to the Internet until they had been premiered at VividCon.[8]

Physical media in the form of DVDs also continued to have a role in the community, despite the dominance of online video distribution. Their main role was at the conventions where all the videos premiered there were given to attendees on a compilation DVD set in their delegate packs, and later mailed out to non-attending delegates. DVDs were seen as superior to online distribution methods in this situation because the community's video makers generally sought to produce their videos with the highest image quality possible, as this was something generally appreciated within the community; and while DVDs were intermediaries that usually transported these images with little perceptible change, online streaming services, such as YouTube, acted as mediators in the ANT sense, distorting and modifying the images they carried. They did this as part of the translation processes of video upload and play back, where online streaming services used bit rates, frame rates, and encoding methods that sacrificed some image quality for various technical and economic benefits related to their hosting operations.

The lack of fidelity of the translations performed by the streaming hosting services was one of the reasons why downloadable versions of the video files were provided in the journal posts announcing them, as mentioned above. While premiering producers would make journal posts after the conventions announcing their videos, providing links to higher quality downloadable versions, DVDs provided a more convenient solution: Downloading premiere videos was a time consuming process, as VividCon 2011 for example premiered 88 videos (which were provided to delegates in a 4-DVD set), and even if one was only interested in downloading a subset of these, it still required visiting each of the individual journal entries and downloading the videos one at a time. Physical media therefore remained a component within the community's macro assemblage, albeit in this very restricted context of the fan conventions.

The topology of the community's micro assemblages. The discussion in this section so far has been organized around the different distribution technologies, and primarily focused on how the community as a whole engaged with them, sometimes using the experiences of individual community members to illustrate this. What this approach elides is the granularity of the community's macro assemblage, that is, the specific details of how individual community members constructed and maintained their micro assemblages within it. To provide some flavour of this, and also to demonstrate the complexity of some of these micro assemblages, this section closes with a brief sketch of the micro assemblage of one community member, Luminosity.

Luminosity used eleven different platforms to distribute her videos during the 2011/12 period of the fieldwork, which included journaling, social networking, video hosting, and other types of platforms. Her choice of platforms primarily reflected both her strategies to maintain the stability of her micro assemblage and her desire to reach different types of audiences. Like other members of the community, for the reasons discussed above related to stability and the desire to use fan-friendly technology, she announced her videos by posting to Dreamwidth and simultaneously cross-posted to LiveJournal. Links to the Dreamwidth journal entries were posted on her Facebook and Twitter accounts primarily to reach the audience in her social network beyond the community. In the latter part of the fieldwork, she also started embedding her videos directly from YouTube within Tumblr and Pinterest, an online pin-up board, to reach other kinds of audiences. Also, while she was not using it regularly, she had also embedded some of her videos within her AO3 account since, like other members, she saw its potential as a permanent repository for the community.

Luminosity's desire for a permanent repository for her videos and their associated elements, such as audience comments, arose from her experience of losing these when the enrolments of hosting platforms she had previously used within her micro assemblage became unstable and failed: Not only did she experience this loss through the closure of iMeem, like many others in the community, but she also experienced it when the hosting platform Stage6 was shut down and when Vimeo suspended her account for a breach in terms of service over a copyright infringement claim.[9] This instability not only arose from the loss of her accounts, but also from changes to the hosting platforms themselves that made them diverge from Luminosity's interests, thus undermining the translations the enrolments were based on. For example, she had used vidders.net, a fan-run hosting platform, but stopped using it when it started to charge a subscription fee, and she had also used Blip, but stopped using it in frustration when she started experiencing long delays between her uploading a video there and it becoming live on the service. Her experiences with all these platforms had eventually led her to reluctantly adopt YouTube during the time of the fieldwork since her perception, like those of some other members in the community discussed above, was that the smaller platforms could not be relied upon for the long term. She did, however, maintain an account on Viddler, another video hosting platform, and also uploaded her videos there to provide redundancy in case YouTube rejected a video or suspended her account, in addition to maintaining her own website, Eyecandy, which contained higher quality downloadable video files.

The Ongoing Challenge of Destabilization Processes

Revisiting the LiveJournal vidding community five years later, I found that they were still contending with many of the destabilization processes discussed above, and some of these had resulted in significant changes. One major change was that the journaling platforms had lost their central position within the community's macro assemblage, which resulted from a combination of factors. One such factor related to the move of fan fiction writers to AO3. While this was already underway in 2011/12, it had reached the point by 2016/17, with AO3 maturing as a platform, where it was being used in preference to the journaling sites by many for various aspects of their fan-related activities, rather than simply alongside them. Since many in the community were also fan fiction readers and writers, this led to a general reduction in the use of the journals by community members.

In addition to AO3, other platforms had risen to prominence within the community, and these were also drawing users away from the journals. Tumblr, for example, was seen by some members as a relatively quick and easy way to remain engaged with the community and other film and television fans compared to the journals: Rather than being a place for lengthy and reflective text-based posts or discussions, the community saw Tumblr as a platform primarily for sharing videos or images, often created by third parties. Also, while the functionality existed within Tumblr to leave text comments, the perception within the community was that using the "reblog" functionality to repost someone else's post into their timeline, or merely clicking on the "like" icon, were acceptable and sufficient forms of feedback.[10] Twitter had also gained prominence within the community and for similar reasons: Its short-format messaging system, coupled with a feedback system similar to Tumblr's in both functionality and community expectations, offered a quick and easy way to remain engaged with other members of the community. While community members using Tumblr and Twitter in 2011/12 would also post to the journals, by 2016/17, given the reduced prominence of the journals due to the shift to AO3 and the increased use of these two platforms within the community, some members believed that it was no longer worth the additional work to post separately on the journals. Some community members had even begun to use Tumblr in preference to the journals to announce their videos.

The decline of LiveJournal's role within the community intensified in April 2017 when it introduced new terms of service that were perceived as hostile to slash fandom by many in the community, resulting in some of them ceasing to use the platform. This event, combined with the increasing appeal of other platforms for some in the community, resulted in a reduction in the number of entries and comments appearing on LiveJournal and Dreamwidth, which had a cascading effect because, as we saw in the previous section, journal entries and comments were actants that interested others to create journal entries and leave comments, and therefore even some of those that still preferred to use the journals reduced their use of them because of this general reduction in activity. Overall, this led to the failure of the translations that connected the different community members together via these platforms, destabilizing the macro assemblage, in spite of the fact that the members' journals remained connected via friends lists: Recalling in this context Latour's (2005, 132) observation that the connections within an assemblage are not durable, but must "be traced anew by the passage of another vehicle, another circulating entity", the macro assemblage had relied upon the circulation of journal entries and comments through the interconnected journaling accounts as one of the stabilization processes that renewed the bonds between the community members.

While other platforms had increased in prominence as the journaling platforms lost their position as the primary spaces of community interaction, none of them had both gained acceptance across the community as a whole and replicated the functionality of the journals that had previously allowed them to stabilize the community's macro assemblage. AO3, for example, while its use was widespread throughout the community, was still perceived as primarily a platform for fan fiction, a perception that was compounded by the fact that the OTW was no longer actively engaged in trying to find video hosting solutions, as its resources were fully occupied managing the growth of fan fiction on the platform, and this had deterred some community members from fully embracing it. In addition, AO3 was an archive, not a social networking platform, and therefore did not replicate the functionality of the journals that allowed for the regular interactions between community members that stabilized the community's macro assemblage. On the other hand, while Tumblr and Twitter were social networking platforms, neither had gained widespread acceptance throughout the community as platforms for sharing and engaging with videos. One main reason for this was that some community members found the video-related posts difficult to find amongst the constant flow of general fan-related posts, personal posts, and reblogs/retweets appearing in their accounts' feeds from the community members they were following. The decline in the journals' use was therefore a deterritorialization process that destabilized the community's macro assemblage as members moved their primary video-related activity from a shared online space, the journals, to different online spaces.[11]

The community was threatened with further deterritorialization as the VividCon organizing committee announced in June 2017 that the 2018 VividCon convention would be the final one, citing falling attendance in recent years as the reason for this (renenet 2017): The organizing committee's view, which was one shared within the community, was that VividCon's founding purpose in 2002 as a place to come to watch and discuss high-quality videos had been undermined by online distribution technologies, which provided various alternative spaces for this that offered community members much more flexibility with respect to when and where they watched and discussed videos and without the time commitment and financial cost of convention attendance. Although some community members still appreciated the face-to-face aspects of VividCon, as discussed above, the organizing committee believed that their numbers were insufficient to support the convention in its traditional form.

In the face of these deterritorialization processes that moved members away from the journals and VividCon, there were indications that in spite of its limitations with respect to video, the community might in fact "reterritorialize" (DeLanda 2006b, 123) on AO3. This process was being driven by community events known as "exchanges": These were events where producers would supply a short list of fandoms for which they were prepared to make a video and where other community members would provide a short list of fandoms for which they would like a video made. The fandoms suitable for inclusion for each event were dictated by the particular theme of that event (for example, space fandoms was one such theme). Individuals from these two groups that shared a fandom on their list in common were anonymously matched with each other, although the identities of both parties were revealed when the event's videos were made public.

AO3 had exchange management functionality built into it in order to manage the fan fiction exchange Yuletide, and this functionality was an actant that interested the vidding community into managing their exchanges on that platform too. This had begun with Equinox, which was an exchange that was scheduled to run twice a year, with the first one occurring between January and April 2017. This event had encouraged some members who had previously been ambivalent about AO3 to give it a more central role in their micro assemblages. In addition, the organizers of Festivids, the video exchange that ran annually from September to January since 2009, announced that it would be moving from Dreamwidth to AO3 for the 2017 and subsequent editions (cosmic_llin 2017). These exchanges were processes that not only stabilized the community by reterritorializing it on AO3, but also by translating the interests of community members, connecting those with common interests in the events' themes and fandoms, potentially either renewing existing connections or creating new ones, thereby helping to maintain or increase the density of the community's connections.

The community in 2016/17 was also still contending with the destabilization processes caused by the video hosting platforms they used. Since 2011/12, both Blip and Viddler joined the growing list of hosting platforms used by the community that had either closed down or had changed their business model so that they no longer accepted the community's videos. In addition, some community members believed Vimeo had taken a less sympathetic position on fair use in recent years, and this had resulted in more takedowns. One particular example of this involved Festivids, which was disrupted one year when Vimeo took down many of the event's videos.

These problems with Blip, Viddler, and Vimeo had encouraged even more community members to adopt YouTube, because of its likely long-term stability, as discussed above. This was in spite of continued misgivings about YouTube, particularly concerning its attitude to fair use, which still left members contending with copyright infringement notices that they consider spurious. In fact, some community members found themselves engaged in protracted translation processes as they tried to stabilize YouTube's enrolment in their assemblages. An example of this was documented by lim (2017), a community member and video maker, and the key aspects of her experience are summarized and analysed here: Immediately after she uploaded her video "Horse", a remix of the television series *Peaky Blinders*, she received a notice from YouTube, which she believed was generated by its Content ID matching system, stating that the BBC and the international television production company Endemol had claimed the copyright for the video, and that as a result it had been blocked in some countries. This notice, and the subsequent difficulties lim experienced contesting it, can be understood, following Callon (1986, 203–214), in the context of the "trials of strength", multilateral negotiations, and strategies that actors engage in over a third party actor when their "problematizations" of a particular situation have conflicting definitions for that actor: While the BBC and Endemol defined "Horse" as their property, lim, in the notice she filed disputing their copyright claim, asserted that the video was in fact her property since she had a right to use these organizations' source material without permission under the fair use provision of copyright law.

Lim's dispute notice was subsequently rejected by the copyright holders, who reiterated their legal claim. The message informing her of this provided an appeal option, which she exercised in spite of its requirements and consequences. These included the requirement that she provide her legal name and contact information, which would be shared with the copyright claimants, along with a legally binding statement asserting her claim over the video. She also ran the risk, in the case of an unsuccessful appeal, that her video would be taken down with her YouTube account accruing one strike. Her appeal was in fact subsequently rejected by the copyright holders, who reasserted their original claim, and lim was notified that her video would be taken down on a certain date, and a copyright strike would be applied to her account. Lim's two attempts to convince the copyright holders that her definition of the video was the correct one had therefore failed, in spite of her enlisting allies in the form of the fair use provisions of copyright law and experts within the community who helped draft the appeal. In the context of these competing problematizations, at this stage of the process at least, YouTube operated as an ally of the copyright holders: The dispute management system required lim to convince the copyright holders that her definition of the video was the correct one, rather than vice versa, and if she was unsuccessful YouTube would apply sanctions against her that would cut the video off from her problematization.

The notice informing lim of her rejected appeal also gave her the option of cancelling it before the takedown date, which would allow the video to remain on YouTube in its current state (that is, blocked in some countries) and also avoid the strike against her account, or the option of filing a copyright counter-notification after the video was taken down. In taking the latter option, she was required to reiterate her fair use claim, make another legally binding declaration, this time under penalty of perjury, and was informed that filing the counter-notification would trigger a legal process that would restore her video, but may result in the copyright holders suing her to remove it. This stage of the process revealed that it was in fact a multilateral negotiation over the video's identity: Her counter-notification was a sworn statement to YouTube that her definition of it was the correct one, and this actant finally allowed her to enrol YouTube as an ally in her conflict with the copyright holders since it acted to both restore the video, cutting the video off from the copyright holder's problematization of it, and also shifted the onus for redefining the video to them. Up to this point, however, YouTube had acted as an ally of the copyright holders by making lim go through a long, convoluted, and, as she described it, "scary" process that was no doubt designed to deter users from reaching that point, a strategy probably conceived to convince copyrights holders that YouTube was in fact aligned with their interests.

Conclusion

For most of the period that the LiveJournal vidding community had been distributing its videos online, it had faced challenges in maintaining the stability of the assemblages that it had constructed for that purpose. The key event of iMeem's decision to no longer host videos in 2009, only two years after the community had adopted that platform en masse, can be seen as the beginning of their ongoing issues concerning finding a stable platform from which to stream their videos, although even before this event some community members were having difficulties with video hosting, such as with the closure of Stage6 in the previous year. The community's producers tried to stabilize their distribution assemblages using various strategies in the face of these difficulties, such as using redundant hosting platforms, choosing larger platforms over the smaller and therefore potentially more precarious ones, and maintaining their own video download sites.

While these strategies helped avoid disruption and loss on the scale of the iMeem event, individual producers still had to contend with the ongoing challenges to the stability of their micro assemblages caused by video hosting platforms through takedowns, account closures, DMCA notices, changes to business models, and their occasional demise. While the community desired a video streaming solution of their own as a way to increase the stability of their assemblages, such a solution remained elusive because of its complexity and because of the scale of resources it required. In spite of the antipathy the community in general had shown towards using YouTube, these different circumstances had eventually led to its widespread adoption: With no option of their own on the horizon, and a deepening scepticism towards the viability and reliability of other hosting platforms, the general success the community had with challenging YouTube's DMCA notices over recent years led them to believe that it was currently the most stable video hosting platform for their needs, despite the work required to maintain its enrolment in their assemblages through responding to those notices. However, with no power to stop an adverse change in either YouTube's current policy or its copyright claims process, the stability of the producers' micro assemblages depended on an actor whose interests, which were ultimately commercial in nature, were not aligned with theirs.

Difficulties with LiveJournal's changing practices and policies, and its occasional technical instability, contributed to the community's disenchantment with it, despite it having been central to their Internet activities even before they began distributing videos online. This, along with the increasing heterogeneity in the community's online communicative practices and the impending demise of its primary offline communal event, were deterritorialization processes that were fragmenting the community's identity. Although reterritorialization processes had begun in response, the likely outcome of these was not clear by the end of the fieldwork, leaving the community's macro assemblage in a precarious state.

Notes

1 Fan fiction, or "fan fic", refers to a style of writing done by fans which uses fictional works, such as television programmes, or famous people, as material for their own fictional works.

2 The email list "vidder" was still active in 2017, and while some informants said that they still occasionally received emails from it, none of them had posted to it for several years.

3 The LiveJournal vidding community members typically used pseudonyms when engaged in fan-related activities and were referred to by these names in conversations and documents as if they were the members' actual names. This is a practice followed here, and these pseudonyms are differentiated in this book from the ones I have provided by not being introduced using the usual style conventions.

4 The Digital Millennium Copyright Act of 1998 is part of US copyright law and contains provisions for parties to issue notices concerning copyright infringement and for notified parties to respond with counter-notices claiming fair use (US Copyright Office 1998).

5 These two components also enacted the DMCA, which too was a document with an expressive role in YouTube's assemblage.

6 Additional context concerning iMeem with respect to fan video making is provided in Chapter 2.

7 These websites were also maintained so as to provide the community with higher quality versions of the videos than those appearing on the third-party platforms.

8 As the name indicates, the VividCon organizers required that for a video to be eligible for showing at any of the premieres sessions it must not have been shown at any other conventions, uploaded to the Internet, or made available publicly in any way.

9 Stage6 was a video hosting service run by DivX Inc. that was shut down for financial reasons in 2008 (DivX 2008).

10 Tumblr counted and aggregated the number of "likes", "reblogs", comments, and "shares" (sending the post directly to someone else on Tumblr) and recorded this total at the bottom of the original post, giving the creator of the post an idea of its impact.

11 The extension of DeLanda's (2006b, 12–13) concept of spatial deterritorialization to include online spaces is discussed in Chapter 4.

References

Archive of Our Own. 2013. *Archive Roadmap 2013*, [cited June 11 2013]. Available from http://archiveofourown.org/admin_posts/295.

Callon, Michel. 1980. "Struggles and Negotiations to Define What Is Problematic and What Is Not: The Socio-Logic of Translation." *The Social Process of Scientific Investigation* no. 4:197–219.

Callon, Michel. 1986. "Some Elements of a Sociology of Translation: The Domestication of the Scallops and St Brieuac Fishermen." In *Power, Action and Belief*, edited by J. Law, 196–232. London: Routledge and Kegan Paul.

cosmic_llin. 2017. *New FAQ and Survey Responses*, [cited September 26 2017]. Available from http://festivids.dreamwidth.org/99151.html.

DeLanda, Manuel. 2006a. "Deleuzian Social Ontology and Assemblage Theory." In *Deleuze and the Social*, edited by M. Fuglsang and B.M. Sørensen, 250–266. Edinburgh: Edinburgh University Press.

DeLanda, Manuel. 2006b. *A New Philosophy of Society: Assemblage Theory and Social Complexity*. London: Continuum (Kindle Edition).

DeLanda, Manuel. 2010. *Deleuze: History and Science*. New York: Atropos.

DeLanda, Manuel. 2016. *Assemblage Theory*. Edinburgh: Edinburgh University Press.

Deleuze, Gilles, and Claire Parnet. 2006. *Dialogues II*. London: Continuum.

DivX, Inc. 2008. *Stage6*. Rovi Corporation, [cited July 22 2013]. Available from www.divx.com/stage6/.

Fanlore. 2017. *Strikethrough and Boldthrough*, [cited August 30 2017]. Available from https://fanlore.org/wiki/Strikethrough_and_Boldthrough#Origin_of_the_Names:_.22Strikethrough.22_and_.22Boldthrough.22.

Latour, Bruno. 1987. *Science in Action: How to Follow Scientists and Engineers through Society*. Cambridge, MA: Harvard University Press.

Latour, Bruno. 2005. *Reassembling the Social*. Oxford: Oxford University Press.

Law, John. 2003. Traduction/Trahison: Notes on ANT. www.lancaster.ac.uk/sociology/research/publications/papers/law-traduction-trahison.pdf.

Law, John. 2009. "Actor Network Theory and Material Semiotics." In *The New Blackwell Companion to Social Theory*, edited by B. Turner, 141–158. Oxford: Wiley-Blackwell.

lim. 2017. *This is Not Legal Advice*, [cited September 29 2017]. Available from https://vidders.github.io/articles/vidding/legal.html.

renenet. 2017. *Major Announcement about the Future of VividCon – Please Read!*, [cited September 22 2017]. Available from http://vividcon.dreamwidth.org/417106.html.

US Copyright Office. 1998. *The Digital Millenium Copyright Act of 1998: U.S. Copyright Office Summary*. Washington, DC: Library of Congress.

6 The California Community Media Exchange
Public Access Television

We saw in the previous two chapters how using Assemblage Theory and ANT to analyse visionOntv and the LiveJournal vidding community allowed for a detailed account of the activities of these two groups, characterizing them as complex, dynamic, and precarious arrangements of, primarily, people and machines. This chapter follows the same approach in its examination of the community media centres and public access television producers that were part of the California Community Media Exchange (CACMX), introduced in Chapter 2.

The first section initially addresses CACMX as a whole and shows that while it was a nascent macro assemblage of community media centres and producers at the beginning of the 2011/12 fieldwork, it destabilized only a few months later. Because of this, the individual centres and the producers associated with them became the focus of the fieldwork, rather than CACMX as a whole. This section will therefore shift focus after the initial discussion of CACMX to present case studies of two centres, Davis Media Access (DMA) and the Community Media Center of Marin (CMCM), with the second section focusing on case studies of three producers associated with these centres, although both sections will also contain insights from some of the other CACMX centres and producers. These first two sections will examine how the producers' public access videos were distributed online by the centres and the producers themselves, analysing the various processes to which these efforts were subject using concepts from Assemblage Theory and ANT. While the analysis of these two sections is based on fieldwork carried out over 2011/12, the third section will draw upon research conducted in 2016/17 to examine how the centres' and producers' distribution activities changed over time.

The Community Media Centres' Distribution of Producer Videos Online

The community media centres in California had been coming under increasing threat due to changes in their funding arrangements in the five years leading up to the 2011/12 period of fieldwork, with many forced to close as a result. CACMX was an association set up in response to this threat with the purpose of sharing best practices and resources between seven community media centres in Northern California. The formation of CACMX had its origins in an initiative funded by the Digital Arts Service Corps, which involved one of their volunteers facilitating its creation in 2010, who then remained to administrate it in its early stages.[1] By 2011, the volunteer was coordinating regular meetings between the staff of the different centres, and she had also facilitated the production of the first of what was planned to be a series of videos focusing on issues relevant to Northern California, which was collaboratively produced by the different centres.

Following DeLanda (2010, 68–69), these activities can be understood as the first emergent properties of the nascent CACMX assemblage and relied upon the interaction of its components: the different community media centres. This was possible because the volunteer was able to bring the staff of the different centres together by translating their interests: According to one formulation of the process of translation within ANT, it involves "offering new interpretations of these interests and channelling people in different directions" (Latour 1987, 117). In this case, persuading members of the stations' staff to postpone their short-term, individual work commitments periodically to attend meetings that addressed their collective, longer-term interests. Also, by applying DeLanda's (2006a, 252, 2010, 69) relativized scaling of assemblages to this situation, if we conceptualize the centres as micro assemblages, CACMX can be understood as a macro assemblage whose purpose was to apply a top-down, stabilizing effect on its component centres (by enabling the sharing of best practices and resources between them).[2]

Midway through 2011, however, the Digital Arts Service Corps had its funding cut and the community media centres were left to continue the development and administration of CACMX on their own. The centres, however, lacked the capacity to take on this additional burden and, therefore, were unable to perform the "constant maintenance work" that Law (2003, 3) identifies as essential to ensuring the stability of an assemblage. As a result, the nascent CACMX macro assemblage did not stabilize, which meant the community media centres generally operated independently of each other for the duration of the 2011/12 fieldwork and, in particular, pursued their own online video distribution strategies for public access television programmes. As a result, they will be addressed individually for the remainder of this section.

Before examining the centres' online video distribution strategies, it is important to understand the relationship that existed between the producers and the centres, as this provides a context for the emergence of these strategies, and those of the producers, which will be discussed in the second section: The centres typically provided materials, facilities, skills, and labour to assist producers in their productions, and this involved the small number of permanent and part-time staff at the centres (typically numbering around six) in training would-be producers in filming, editing, and studio production techniques. The staff were also involved in maintaining and managing the facilities and equipment used by the producers, such as television studios, editing suites, and video cameras. In addition, the staff sometimes helped the producers make their programmes (such as directing studio shows or operating cameras), although this was mostly done by volunteers from the local community who were either sourced by the staff or the producers. While some producers did not avail themselves of these resources, others did, with some of this latter category unable to produce their videos without them.

The public access producers were not part of the centres' organizations, but were rather members of the general public who lived within their catchment area. Their interactions with the centres varied depending on their output level, show format, and their need for the centres' resources: For example, some producers visited the centres a few times a week over the period while they were working on a show or receiving training, while others with episodic studio productions visited every month or two for a few hours. Some producers had never visited the centres, such as some religious groups who used their own equipment and posted the shows to the centres on DVDs. Some producers had relationships going back for a decade or more, while others only visited once, or made one show, and had no further contact with the centres. The producers at any given centre also typically operated independently of each other.

While the producers often made their own arrangements for distributing their videos online, which will be addressed in the next section, the centres also distributed the producers' videos. The various CACMX centres emphasized different reasons for doing this, and DMA's motivation was to provide an accessible video archive of the local community of Davis for that community, as well as to meet what they believed was the growing expectation within the community that public access television be available online.

DMA had previously experimented with YouTube, Blip, and Vimeo, but ultimately they did not regard commercial third party video platforms as suitable for their needs, and so did not use them to distribute the producers' video. One reason for this was that DMA was a non-commercial entity, and they believed that this identity should be maintained in the Internet era, and so excluding these platforms from DMA was, following DeLanda (2006b, 12), a territorialization process to maintain its homogeneity. The exclusion of these platforms was also an acknowledgement by DMA that the commercial interests of their owners and operators made it difficult, if not impossible, to redefine these platforms in a non-commercial way. For example, DMA did not have the ability to prevent advertising appearing in the same pages as the producers' videos on these platforms. Also, even if a platform was acceptable to DMA in its present form with respect to its commerciality, it may undergo changes over time, and DMA would have very little power to influence this. In short, applying Callon's (1986, 207) formulation of the translation process, DMA acknowledged that it did not have the power to win the "trials of strength" or negotiations required to redefine these platforms in ways that conflicted with the definitions given to them by their owners and operators. DMA also had concerns that the enrolment of such platforms into their distribution assemblage would be precarious, since these platforms could close down at any time, and this contributed to DMA's reasons for avoiding them: They did not have the resources to go through the process of uploading the hundreds of videos they envisaged making available online to a replacement hosting platform in the event of a closure.

As an alternative to the commercial video hosting platforms, DMA had developed their own platform. This involved embedding videos into their website Davis Community Television (DCTV) from a video-on-demand server that they maintained themselves. For their programmes to be available on this platform, a producer first had to provide a DMA staff member with a video file, and then that staff member would encode it into an mp4 format file and upload it to the video-on-demand server. The staff member would also encode the producer's file into an mpeg2 format so that it was compatible with DMA's cable television system, Cablecast, which was responsible for broadcasting their public access channel through the city of Davis's cable television network, and also upload the file to that system. In addition, the staff member also needed to create a record for the programme and include the appropriate metadata (including such things as the producer's name and the show's title) within it as part of the video upload process.

During the 2011/12 period of the fieldwork, DMA were in the process of developing and implementing a new platform: This was based on a content management system that was part of the Open Media Project (OMP), which was as an open-source set of tools based on the Drupal content management system. The OMP was being developed by a group of community media centres, which included DMA as the only CACMX centre in the group, with the objective of reducing the amount of time staff spent on basic tasks through a combination of allowing the producers to do these themselves through the Internet and automating them. For example, the OMP, when complete, would allow producers to create show records, enter metadata, and upload videos of their programmes to the platform. The OMP, when fully integrated into Cablecast, would then take the videos uploaded by the producers and automatically encode and upload them with the associated metadata to both the Cablecast system and the video-on-demand server for the DCTV website. The development and integration of the OMP was a process intended to stabilize

DMA in the face of possible reductions to their funding. When complete, it would do this by helping them maintain their current operations in the event of any cost cutting forced upon them by increasing their staff's capacity by removing staff from basic tasks, such as enrolling the producers' videos into their distribution assemblage, by shifting the work of translation onto the producers and the OMP.

The development and integration of the OMP proved to be a long and complex process, however, and by the end of the 2011/12 fieldwork, the new distribution assemblage was still not stable enough to replace the existing one. One important factor contributing to this was that the new assemblage was not sufficiently "coded". Coding is a process involving language in stabilizing an assemblage (DeLanda 2010, 13), and in the case of DMA, lack of time and resource for the development team meant that the staff and producers trialling the new assemblage were not receiving sufficient training in the OMP tools, and supporting documentation was lacking. Software bugs within the OMP also acted to decode the assemblage further, as these sometimes required revising procedures, making elements of the limited existing documentation and training materials obsolete. Producers and staff trialling the tools were therefore sometimes using the tools incorrectly, and this sometimes destabilized the assemblage by causing it to malfunction.

While DMA believed that it was part of its remit as a community media centre to make the public access television producers' videos available online, in addition to broadcasting them on the cable television network, it did not have the resources to develop DCTV into a space for audience discussion and interaction beyond providing basic commenting functionality. DMA believed instead that their limited resources were best used to create an archive of videos that audiences could search through, via the metadata, and to provide functionality to enable them to share and discuss the videos on their existing social networking sites, such as Facebook. This was an acknowledgement by DMA that they did not have the resources or the expertise to be able to develop DCTV into a site that would be able to interest audiences in interacting with the videos and each other there. They were content instead for DCTV to be an actor that simply allowed users to enrolled the producers' videos into the users' existing social networking assemblages. Therefore, DMA did not attempt to stimulate conversations around the videos on DCTV, nor were they concerned by the fact that there were very few comments left on videos on the DCTV website.

CMCM's reason for distributing their public access producers' videos online was to allow them to be seen outside of Marin County's cable television network. Their platform for doing this was Miro Community, a free, open source video aggregation software platform developed and distributed by the Participatory Culture Foundation, which was embedded within the centre's website. The producers were granted permission by CMCM to set up accounts on the platform, and this allowed them to link their videos, hosted elsewhere, to Miro Community via an RSS feed. Miro Community did not automatically publish the videos, but queued them pending approval by a CMCM staff member, and this approval was only withheld if the videos did not conform to the general restrictions on public access television content (such as containing offensive or commercial material), or if they had yet to be shown on the cable television channel.

One reason CMCM had been initially attracted to Miro Community was because it did not require them to take on the cost and work of hosting videos, while still allowing them control over what appeared on their website. However, unlike DMA, because they did not take on this responsibility, they needed strategies to interest producers in linking their videos to CMCM's website. One such strategy related to their choice of Miro Community: CMCM considered its aesthetics, usability, and functionality on a par with commercial video hosting platforms and believed therefore it would be attractive to producers. Another strategy involved CMCM extending their original remit as a community media centre to train local people in film making techniques, such as camera use and editing, to include classes on the use of video distribution technologies, such as Miro Community and the hosting platforms producers might use with it. The choice of Miro Community and the classes were therefore partly translation processes, where CMCM attempted to translate the producers' interest in creating and distributing their videos into one that included the CMCM website as part of this.

While many of CMCM's producers did in fact choose to include the CMCM website, and hence Miro Community, within their distribution assemblages, its enrolment proved to be unstable. Similar to DeLanda's (2006b, 82) example of the US computer manufacturing industry discussed in Chapter 3, video hosting and distribution technology was in a rapid state of flux during the period of the 2011/12 fieldwork, and because the various organizations involved in developing it innovated and responded to technological changes in different ways and at different speeds, this dynamic aspect of the technology increased its heterogeneity and therefore constituted a "deterritorialization" process (DeLanda 2006b, 12) that CMCM had to contend with. One example concerned Blip, which was a video hosting platform used by many of CMCM's producers (for reasons that will be addressed in the next section). At one point during the fieldwork, Blip had begun supporting high definition videos, but these were not compatible with Miro Community. While CMCM were eventually able to perform an ad hoc modification to Miro Community to rectify this, they believed that the developers at Miro Community needed to perform more fundamental modifications to the platform to provide a more stable solution. On another occasion, Blip updated its platform in such a way that videos hosted on it were no longer appearing on Miro Community. On this occasion, CMCM did not have the resources available to find a solution, although Blip eventually provided another update that rectified the problem. The dynamic nature of these technologies also destabilized the producers' enrolment by making the training they received in them increasingly obsolete over time, and this also meant that the CMCM staff had to devote time to rewriting training materials and retraining producers.

Examples such as these highlighted for CMCM the precariousness of their website's enrolment within the producers' online distribution assemblages. The disparity of resources between the commercial hosting platforms, on the one hand, and CMCM and the Miro Community development team, on the other, restricted their ability to counter the ongoing deterritorialization processes brought about by the rapid changes in online video technology. By the end of the 2011/12 fieldwork, CMCM were considering various stabilization strategies. One was to commit to Miro Community for the longer term and devote substantial resource to its development and maintenance, but the ongoing work required to achieve this was prohibitive, especially given CMCM's limited funding and the fact that its primary remit was to develop and operate the cable television aspect of the centre. CMCM had also considered using the OMP as an alternative, but had rejected it: Unlike DMA, they saw their platform as a destination for audiences and, therefore, believed that any replacement for Miro Community would need to have the aesthetics and functionality of commercial platforms to interest audiences in its use as a destination, which the OMP did not have in their opinion. They also did not believe that the OMP was sufficiently appealing to interest producers in its use either, which was an important consideration, since CMCM did not want the replacement platform to require them to take on the extra work involved in uploading, hosting, and linking to the producers' video themselves.

The Producers' Use of the Internet as a Video Distribution Technology

As mentioned above, the public access television producers operated independently of their associated community media centres and of each other. Also, the kinds of videos they made, the reasons they made them, and their reasons and methods for distributing their videos online varied significantly. Therefore, to reflect these individual and diverse circumstances, this section will primarily be organized around a selection of case studies that will give a flavour for the way these kinds of producers operated online. The application of the theoretical concepts from Chapter 3 to these will mostly be deferred until the end of the section, where they will be applied to the three case studies together and to the experiences of some other producers associated with the CACMX centres, where these concepts will provide a framework to compare the experiences of the different producers.

The first case study concerns Frank, a resident of Davis who worked primarily as a DJ and who had been affiliated with DMA for over a decade. His reasons for producing television programmes were two-fold: To use them to provide a positive role model for local youth and, secondarily, as promotional tools showcasing his skills to help him gain contract work as a video maker to supplement his income. He did this through producing programmes that mostly concerned the local hip-hop music culture.

Frank had an ambivalent attitude towards the Internet as a video distribution technology. He believed it was important for him to distribute his videos online because it allowed him to promote his work outside Davis and because he believed his television audience had an expectation that his videos should also be available online. However, he struggled with, and was frustrated by, some of the technologies he used to try and achieve this. For example, he had set up a YouTube channel in 2009, but stopped using it during the period of the 2011/12 fieldwork because many of the videos he uploaded to it were either being taken down or not appearing at all. He believed the reason for this was because his videos contained concert performances of the hip-hop artists he interviewed that YouTube mistakenly believed he did not have permission to use. Framing this situation in terms of Callon's (1986, 207) notion of competing problematizations, YouTube provided producers with an actor, its dispute resolution mechanism, that they could enrol as an ally into their assemblages to help stabilize the enrolment of their videos in such circumstances by using it to demonstrate to YouTube and copyright holders that the producers' definition of the video as something complaint with copyright law was in fact the correct one. In Frank's case, however, he was not aware of the existence of this mechanism, and did not recall ever receiving a notice from YouTube concerning copyright infringement, and therefore his perceived inability to stabilize YouTube within his assemblage prompted him to look for alternative video hosting platforms. Another difficulty Frank had with YouTube concerned the length of videos it allowed him to upload. His public access television programmes were around 30 minutes in length, but YouTube was limiting him to 15 minutes during the period of the fieldwork, which had increased from 10 minutes in the preceding years. This limitation of YouTube had in fact changed the way Frank made his videos: Rather than continuing to make the longer form public access programmes and breaking them up, he started making some shorter format videos he could upload in one piece.

Frank had originally used MySpace as a way of widening his audience, alongside YouTube, and was attracted to it because of its music orientation. By the time of the 2011/12 fieldwork however, its loss of users to other social media platforms, along with its decreased emphasis on music, meant that he was no longer actively using it. Because of these issues with YouTube and MySpace, Frank had turned to Facebook. While he had maintained a Facebook page for his video production activities a year before the fieldwork, he had only recently started to directly upload his videos there, rather than simply providing links to YouTube from Facebook posts. Frank believed Facebook had more lenient terms of services with respect to copyright for videos and he, in fact, did not have any issues during the period of the fieldwork. Facebook also allowed a longer duration for videos uploaded to it at that time than YouTube did.

Facebook, however, presented a different stabilization problem for Frank: While he saw Facebook as a more stable component for his assemblage than YouTube, and one that enabled him to enrol more videos than YouTube and enrol a larger audience than MySpace, he believed he needed to make regular posts concerning his video-making activities, and to respond to the comments he received on his posts, to maintain his Facebook audience. These posts and comments are the "circulating entities" Latour (2005, 132) sees as essential to maintaining the stability of an assemblage, travelling from Frank's computer to the screens of his audience on a regular basis. However, he sometimes found this ongoing maintenance work burdensome and a distraction from spending time finding paying gig work through more fruitful avenues, to the point where he took his Facebook account offline for a few weeks on two occasions during the fieldwork. This activity on Facebook was aimed at maintaining his audience, rather than trying to form an online community around his videos. He in fact had no interest in the social networking aspects of Facebook, or of YouTube and MySpace for that matter, and merely saw them as "broadcasting stations" for his videos.

Frank saw his use of Facebook to host videos as temporary until he was able to have his own website built, which for him was an important aspect of his distribution strategy, as he did not want third parties restricting what videos he could show, even though he had had no specific issues with Facebook in this regard. This site was in development over the whole period of the fieldwork and was being built by an acquaintance of Frank's in his spare time, although Frank abandoned his plans for it by the end of the fieldwork as the acquaintance was unable to free up enough time, and Frank did not have the funds to pay someone to complete it. While the DCTV website offered a ready-made alternative hosting platform to Facebook, since Frank's videos, like those of all the DMA producers, were eventually uploaded to it by the centre's staff, it did not offer Frank the control and freedom he desired. Therefore, by the end of the fieldwork, Frank's distribution activities were dependent on Facebook, a platform he had very little control over and one that he perceived as requiring effort to maintain which he could ill afford, leaving him with a distribution assemblage that fell short of his needs.

The second case study concerns Deborah, a retiree and a resident of Davis. She primarily produced environmental videos, as well as videos about a variety of social and political issues in Davis and Sacramento. The environmental videos were produced under the banner of her non-profit organization, Environmental Voices, whose mission was "to help preserve our future by providing education and research about toxic chemicals and how they affect our health and the environment", which it did mainly through the production and distribution of videos (Environmental Voices 2010). Deborah saw the Internet as an inexpensive way to reach an audience beyond Davis and beyond the environmentalist events she occasionally screened her videos at elsewhere in the US, and she also believed that there was an expectation amongst her audience that her videos be available online.

Deborah used YouTube as she was not aware of the existence of alternative video hosting platforms at the time she adopted it in 2008. She had some difficulties using the platform, and one such difficulty concerned the limitation YouTube imposed on video lengths. Deborah wanted to distribute her and other producers' environmental documentaries on her YouTube channel, but these were longer than the 15 minutes duration that YouTube allowed her, with some running as long as 90 minutes. She was confused as to why she was not able to upload these videos in their entirety, since she had seen videos on YouTube of similar length.[3] This caused her some frustration during the uploading process and eventually required her to segment documentaries into a series of shorter length videos. Even once cut down, she still found the process of uploading the individual videos technically difficult, and this was no doubt compounded by some shortcomings in the YouTube uploading process at the time, which had been reported by several informants during the fieldwork, resulting in repeated failed uploads, and by the limited time she was able to spend using her computer due to health reasons. While Deborah had in fact learnt how to shoot and edit videos through classes taught by DMA, she lamented that they did not offer classes on uploading. Since she did not have the money to pay other people to upload her videos, she had sought out volunteers, but finding a volunteer for this task had proved difficult, which meant that she had a number of completed videos that had not been uploaded for some months. Separately, her most recent documentary, *Breaking Ground for Peace*, which she had co-produced with others, was uploaded to Vimeo by one of her collaborators, and was also hosted on the website of the organization I Am Peace, which was another of her collaborators.

While Deborah set up and managed an Environmental Voices Facebook page, and appreciated its potential importance for promoting her activities, she in fact used it very little because of the limited time she had to devote to computer-related activities: It contained only a few posts, and these linked to other producers' environmental videos, to audio recording of her radio appearances, and some contained other environmentally related material, although she did not post any of her own videos there. She also had a dormant Environmental Voices MySpace page, which only contained a few stills from one of her documentaries, and an Environmental Voices website, which was not updated during the duration of the fieldwork. The website contained a variety of texts, images, links, and videos concerning environmental matters, although only one of the videos was hers, which was the first 10 minutes of a documentary embedded from YouTube.

Deborah did not have any interest in creating an online community around her videos, nor did she have the time or inclination to engage in online discussions concerning them. She was also not interested in receiving comments on her videos and had disabled comments on YouTube because she felt that negative comments would discourage her from putting her work online. In fact, the development of an online audience was not her primary motivation for making her videos available online, but she rather saw her videos and associated online presence as a resource to support her offline environmental activism: For Deborah, these online sites were primarily places she could direct the people she engaged with at offline forums, such as environmental activist events and meetings and her radio interviews, if they wanted more information about the topics she was discussing.

She did feel, however, that the Internet offered her the opportunity to make more controversial videos in the future: She wanted to make documentaries that were exposés of the political establishment in California, but had avoided making them in the past because of the harm they might do DMA. This was because she produced her videos using DMA's equipment, and therefore they had to be shown on DMA's public access television channel, and eventually uploaded to DCTV, as per DMA's policy discussed earlier. She felt, however, that once she had her own equipment, she would be free to make these kinds of documentaries, because they could then be distributed online through her own platforms, bypassing DMA.

The final case study concerns Antonio, a health practitioner, yoga teacher, and resident of Marin County, who produced the series *YogiViews* at CMCM. His purpose in making the series was "to spread the word of Yoga", and he did this through a series of dialogues with guests who themselves were experts in various aspects of Yoga. Each episode was typically 30 minutes long, and they were usually produced in the CMCM studio with a crew of from four to six volunteers. He uploaded his series to the Internet because he wanted it to reach an audience beyond CMCM's cable television footprint. He had also hoped to make a financial return from his videos in the future, if online video platforms ever introduced revenue models that were funded by subscriptions or charged per view or download, but he believed that the existing advertising-funded models would alienate his audience, and so he did not take up that option.

Antonio uploaded full-length episodes to Blip and then embedded them in several places: The CMCM website, his own *YogiViews* Word-Press site, and his *YogiViews* Facebook page. He used Blip in preference to YouTube for this because he wanted to upload his programmes as a single video file, since when he began *YogiViews* YouTube videos could not be more that 10 minutes in duration. Even though Blip did not require him to cut up his video files into smaller segments, he did believe using the Internet to distribute his videos required him to change his programmes' production aesthetic to be more appealing to an Internet audience, due to the smaller screen sizes of computers and phones compared to television screens. As a result, he used much tighter head shots with no head space for his interviews to make sure he maximized the use of the smaller screens. Antonio did maintain a small YouTube presence, however. While he generally believed that the social networking function of Facebook was superior to that of YouTube, he also believed YouTube's recommendation pane could help bring *YogiViews* to the attention of people who were watching other Yoga-related videos.[4] The videos on his YouTube channel were tailored to this, comprising mostly trailers and highlights of shows around three minutes long made especially for the Internet, which contained his WordPress site's URL in the description section.

Antonio also selected the different platforms he used based on the kinds of audiences he was trying to attract for his videos and on the types of interactions he wanted to have with them concerning those videos. He felt that while YouTube brought with it a general audience, the CMCM website attracted a more sophisticated one that was interested in thoughtful topics. Although he valued the social networking functionality of Facebook and its potential for interacting with audiences and building an online community around his videos, the audience it brought was limited to people he knew, so he also employed WordPress. Antonio felt that WordPress offered a better space for engaging with audiences about his videos than Blip or the CMCM website because it allowed each episode to be viewed within the context of a dedicated *YogiViews* website, which included an archive of all his episodes embedded within it, along with a detailed text background for each episode, as well as background on him and the series. He also believed it had an advantage over Facebook in that the people commenting on WordPress were not previously known to him, and he found their comments offered a fresh perspective on his work, as they were based on the videos they just viewed, rather than being framed by their relationship with Antonio or by the relationships they may have had with his other Facebook friends.

Contrary to his hopes, however, Antonio had very little online interaction with his audience on WordPress or on any of the other platforms he used. The place these interactions occurred most was on Facebook, and he believed this was because it was primarily designed as a place to interact, and therefore encouraged it and made it a natural part of using the site. He, however, found these Facebook interactions of limited value, not only for the reason mentioned above concerning how the interactions were framed, but also because he felt Facebook encouraged only positive comments, and he would have liked it to at least have had a "dislike" button, so his audience could give a more critical assessment of his videos. Also, while he did get a few comments through his Word-Press site, he was overwhelmed by the spam comments he received there and he had in fact stopped reading them altogether as a result, lamenting that WordPress didn't have a better way of filtering these out.

Overall, Antonio was generally disappointed with the very slow pace with which his online audience was building. He attributed possible causes to both the niche subject matter of his videos and his failure to use Internet technology to market them better, due to lack of time, resources, and specialist knowledge. For instance, he had run a Google Ads campaign previously with the help of a volunteer who worked in marketing, and while he felt this was successful, he did not feel able to run such a campaign on his own, nor commit the necessary time and resources to it, and he was reluctant to trouble the volunteer again with this task.

We can see from the above that these three public access producers drew upon various components to create the assemblages that they believed they needed to achieve their goals as video makers. This strategy was in fact typical amongst the other CACMX producers who were informants for this study. It reflected the fact that no single component on its own had all the characteristics or features to provide them with the agency they required. For example, for Antonio to build the size and kind of audience he wanted, and for him to be able to have the interactions he wanted with them, required him to use several different kinds of components interacting with each other in different ways. Even while some aspects of these individual components worked the way the producers required, others needed to undergo translations so that they could coexist with each other in the assemblages. Sometimes this was as simple as disabling the comments section on a YouTube video, but sometimes it required more work, as we saw with the producers who wanted to use YouTube to host their programmes but were required to transform them either by cutting their videos up into smaller components or by changing the way they made their programmes. Many of the CACMX producers used Blip as their primary video hosting platform instead of YouTube because it did not require this additional translational work, although some, such as the producer of the music programme *Spilly Chile's "Bowl of Rocks"* at Community Television, the CACMX community media centre for Santa Cruz county, lamented that she did not have the time to cut her videos into smaller segments to upload to YouTube so as to attract a bigger audience. In fact, as we saw, the agency of the producers' assemblages was significantly constrained by the burden of work required to construct and maintain them, either because of its volume or technical nature, underscoring Latour's observations (in Gane 2004, 83) concerning the centrality of the notion of work to the concept of assemblages. While all three producers in the case studies tried to enrol volunteers to assist with this work, they had limited success in achieving this, and this reliance on volunteers rather than paid labour highlights one of the power asymmetries that exist between non-professional producers and their professional counterparts. Related to this, and also as an example of DeLanda's (2010, 69) arguments concerning the top-down effects of an assemblage on its components, while Deborah's enrolment *within* DMA's assemblage provided her with essential video-making resources which she did not otherwise have access to, thus enabling her video-making activities, it also simultaneous constrained her activities, something that would not have been the case if she had sufficient resources to acquire the equipment and training she needed.

Some producers, such as the one who produced *Look Mom, I'm On TV* at Community Television in Santa Cruz, did not in fact believe the benefits of being online outweighed the extra work required to do so, and therefore were content for their programmes to be broadcast over the cable television network alone. Other producers, on the contrary, would not have made public access television at all if it were not possible to distribute videos online: The producer of *Aspect Ratio* at CMCM, for example, who made his programmes as an education resource for high school film teachers, thought the video-on-demand capability of the Internet was a critical element of his distribution assemblage, since it enabled teachers to access his programmes quickly and easily when they required them, and he believed that teachers would be much less likely to show his programmes in class if they were only available via broadcast television.

The Changing Nature of the Centres' and Producers' Assemblages

The situation with regard to CACMX in 2016/17 remained unchanged from 2011/12: With the departure of the Digital Arts Service Corps volunteer in 2011 and the ongoing constraints on the individual centres' resources and finances, there was no one available to take on the role of coordinator between the centres, and as a result they continued to have very little contact with each other in the intervening years, and continued to operate as separate entities. Because of this, as in the first section, the centres will be addressed individually here, focusing again on DMA and CMCM.

DMA's approach to distributing producers' videos had changed considerably since 2011/12: Funding for the development of the OMP had come to an end, and so work on it had mostly come to a halt. DMA had continued to work on one element of it themselves, which was a reservation system for equipment and facilities booking, but the other aspects of it, including those that allowed the producers to upload their videos to DMA's system, were no longer being developed. DMA had continued to explore others ways to allow producers to upload videos simultaneously to their DCTV video-on-demand server and their Cablecast system, but this continued to prove difficult to implement. The primary issue was that the Cablecast system would only play out a very limited set of file types, and DMA had not found an affordable, automated solution that could check, and transcode where necessary, the many potential video file types the producers might upload to the system to ensure their compatibility with Cablecast.

This situation was eventually overtaken by other events however: As the number of videos DMA hosted increased, so did the work required to maintain their existing video-on-demand platform, and this increase in work had eventually reached a point where it was no longer feasible for DMA to continue to host these videos on this platform. In addition, DMA believed that mobile devices were becoming a major platform for audiences to view Internet videos, but their existing platform did not support this, and so these factors combined prompted DMA to consider alternative hosting arrangements. Around the same time, YouTube had begun offering non-profit organizations accounts that allowed them to upload videos of any length, with the guarantee that they would not be commercialized in any way (for example, no advertising would be inserted into their video streams). An added attraction of YouTube for DMA was that it supported mobile devices. DMA had therefore decided to stop developing their own video-on-demand platform and adopt YouTube in its place, embedding the videos from YouTube into the DCTV website. DMA nonetheless had some reservations about this, and in particular the consequences of having to move platforms again if YouTube changed its policy towards non-profit organizations at some later date.

DMA did not have a feasible way of integrating YouTube into their Cablecast system however, and so they were still left with the work of having to upload the producers' videos twice. This was partially offset by DMA allowing producers who wanted to host their videos themselves to embed them into DCTV from the third-party hosting platforms they used. In spite of this, some producers were not linking their videos to DCTV, either because the producers did not have the time to do it or because they were not interested in using it to distribute their videos. To counter this, and maintain DCTV as a comprehensive community archive for public access television in Davis (containing, as it did, the older videos that were still hosted on the legacy in-house video-on-demand server), a DMA staff member would eventually follow up with these producers asking them to email the links to their videos from the hosting platforms they used, and the staff member would embed these into the DCTV website within the appropriate show record.

DMA's experience can be analysed as a series of processes that worked to both stabilize and destabilize its online video distribution assemblage: The attempted integration of the OMP tool set into DMA's assemblage was a stabilization process that ultimately failed because the OMP itself was a precarious assemblage of software, the community media centres that were developing the tools, and the financial actors that sustained this activity that eventually came apart. DMA continued to try to find ways of removing their staff members from the translation process that allowed producers' videos to coexist with both Cablecast and their video-on-demand server, but without the OMP, this was not possible given the resources available, and the situation was further complicated by the destabilization of their video-on-demand server. In the meantime, YouTube had sufficiently aligned their interests with those of non-profit organizations that DMA felt enrolling it within their assemblage would no longer destabilize its non-commercial identity, at least not in the short term, and that it would in fact stabilize the assemblage overall. While this new arrangement helped stabilize DMA's assemblage by having YouTube take on the burden of video hosting and of maintaining the enrolment of audiences as they moved to mobile devices, the removal of DMA staff from the translation process between the producers' videos and DCTV brought about by this new arrangement introduced a new source of instability: DCTV did not interest some producers enough for them to enrol it into their assemblage, which required DMA staff to take on the burden of this process themselves so they could maintain the identity of their assemblage as a comprehensive local community archive.

CMCM were also undergoing major changes in the way that they distributed their producers' videos online during the 2016/17 fieldwork, and they were not in fact distributing them at all during this period since they were still in the process of implementing their new strategy for this. The catalyst for this change was the decision by the Participatory Culture Foundation to no longer distribute or support Miro Community, which was announced by them without warning or explanation during the period leading up to the 2016/17 fieldwork. With no obvious replacement for it, the CMCM staff began to explore alternatives. The option of working with the developer communities online who were attempting to continue to maintain and develop Miro Community after it was dropped by the Participatory Culture Foundation was ruled out by CMCM because it was believed this would absorb too much of the centre's resources.

CMCM also considered other alternatives, but none allowed for the migration of the existing website structure and metadata without a considerable amount of work. Because CMCM's funding was tied to the broadcast of public access television, they could not justify the cost this would entail, especially since these alternatives would only be temporary, as they would eventually be replaced by the new version of the Cablecast system hardware CMCM were planning to install: This new version, unlike the version both they and DMA used in 2016/17, was designed to automatically create both a cable television broadcast file and a video-on-demand file from a single video file uploaded to it and then copy the video-on-demand file to an integrated Internet server and embed it within a webpage. While the new system did not preserve the original website structure or metadata either, it did allow previously aired programmes to be automatically copied to the video-on-demand server when they were shown again, although ones that were not shown again would have to be uploaded manually by the CMCM staff. Also, the CMCM staff would have to seek copyright approval for online distribution from the producers of these previously aired programmes, since the agreements with producers using the older system did not include these rights, as CMCM did not directly distribute producers' videos previously (since the producers themselves linked their videos into the CMCM website, as discussed in the first section above).

Waiting for this hardware upgrade meant, however, that CMCM did not distribute their producers' videos online for a considerable amount of time, although they were not particularly concerned by this since in 2016/17 they did not consider this as central to their role as a community media centre. Instead, they saw their role as one that built up the skills of producers through training so that they would become self-sufficient with regard to hosting, distributing, and promoting their videos, with the CMCM website made available to them only as a secondary platform.

Framing CMCM's situation using DeLanda's (2006b, 30, 2011, Appendix) concept of diagrams, we can locate their online distribution assemblage before the loss of Miro Community within the space of potential configurations that assemblages of this kind can possibly take, which also includes points within it that represent actual historical examples of such assemblages, including CMCM's in 2011/12. The loss of Miro Community meant, however, that the assemblage's remaining components (such as producers, videos, third-party hosting platforms, RSS feeds, CMCM webpages, and the metadata generated by Miro Community) no longer "co-functioned" (Deleuze and Parnet 2006, 52), and this loss therefore constituted an absolute deterritorialization of the assemblage, meaning that it was no longer described by the diagram, as it was now simply a collection of components with no emergent properties, rather than an assemblage.[5] While CMCM explored potential "reterritorialization" processes (DeLanda 2006b, 123) to stabilize the situation to prevent this, these were not considered feasible, and they instead accepted the coming apart of their assemblage until a new component arrived, which would allow it to be reassembled with a different configuration in the future.

The state of the online video distribution practices of the public access television producers in 2016/17 continued to reflect their specific circumstance, although there were some common themes. The closure of Blip in 2015 by its Disney-owned parent company Maker Studios caused problems for many producers given its widespread use amongst them. Also, around this time, YouTube removed the limitations concerning the length of videos that could be uploaded there, meaning it was able to accept the longer format public access programmes, which saw its adoption as a replacement for Blip by many of the producers as a result. It also meant, however, that the producers had to undertake the work of uploading their videos again and that the videos of producers who used Blip as their sole hosting platform and who had become inactive leading up to its closure were no longer available on the Internet.

While this change to YouTube allowed public access television programmes to be uploaded to it in their original, broadcast form, some producers still decided to change their programmes' formats for it. For example, Sam produced *Artist's Connection*, a monthly series made at DMA that interviewed local artists, with each episode including three interviews and typically running for an hour. After a few months of operation, Sam decided, after gaining feedback from various sources, that the programme was too long for what he perceived as his YouTube audience, and so he changed the format to include only one interview per episode, which ran for around 20 minutes. He believed that his current television audience was very small, and so he was not concerned by the impact that changes to the format might have on it as he expected this would be offset by an increase in his YouTube audience, which was his main concern because of its potential size. These changes did in fact bring a modest increase in the programme's views, likes, and positive comments on YouTube.

Other public access producers had also begun prioritizing Internet distribution over that of cable television. For example, Frank, from the 2011/12 case study in the previous section, had stopped making hip-hop programmes at DMA and was now running a non-profit organization called the Future Development Youth Center that, amongst other things, trained local youth, particularly those from disadvantaged backgrounds, in video production. While this organization maintained some links with DMA, Frank did not believe the youth involved in his training programmes, nor those likely to watch the videos they produced, watched television, so broadcasting them via Davis's cable television network was not a priority for him, and he instead used the organization's YouTube channel as the primary outlet.

With the demise of Blip, Vimeo was the main alternative to YouTube used by public access producers, but it had proved problematic for some. For example, Ginger produced the environmental series *GMO Education* at CMCM and had used Vimeo for the series until she received a notification from them saying that all her videos would be taken down. No explanation was given for this, but Ginger believed that it was due to a combination of factors, including her decision to disable advertising on her videos (since, like many of the public access producers and centres, she believed it was not appropriate to commercialize her videos) and because she was hosting a large number of videos on there that were not getting high numbers of views. In all, Ginger estimated that she had 75 videos taken down. She had adopted Archive.org as her replacement platform, as she believed its remit as a non-commercial archive meant that the likelihood of them taking her videos down was small, but she still had not found the time, years later, to upload all the videos that had previously been taken down.

While the use of social media was acknowledged by producers as a way to promote their videos, the work involved in maintaining an active social media presence proved sufficiently daunting for some that they avoided using it, and this also extended to not having the time to respond to comments on the hosting platforms. Some of those that did take the time to use social media platforms found them problematic, however. For example, Sam of *Artist's Connection* tried to use the programme's Facebook page to promote new episodes, but he found that if he did not pay to "boost" these posts, then they did not reach many of the page's followers. He also tried various other strategies, such as using Facebook's messaging system to contact the page's followers individually, but after sending a number of messages like this, he was notified by Facebook that he was not using the messaging system in a way that it was intended to be used, and as a result his account was suspended for a week. As an alternatively strategy, Sam used Facebook's event feature that allowed up to 500 people to be invited to an event to promote each new video, but he believed his users where receiving many event notifications and therefore they were just being ignored. Ultimately, he stopped trying to use Facebook to directly promote his episodes, and instead encouraged his followers to subscribe to the programme's YouTube channel, since it provided unfiltered notifications to every subscriber each time a new video was uploaded to the channel.

We can see from the above that the stability and configuration of the producers' distribution assemblages depended heavily on the policies and changing circumstances of the platforms they used, over which they had no control: Blip's closure, Vimeo's takedowns, YouTube's change of upload policy, and the differences between how Facebook and YouTube handled notifications reflected their specific circumstances as actors in the media industry and were no doubt consequences of the economic, technological, and strategic constraints that both they and their parent organizations operated under, leaving the producers, as much less powerful actors, to adapt as best they could.

Conclusion

Without the top-down homogenizing effects on the individual centres' micro assemblages that may have emerged from a more stable and longer-lived CACMX macro assemblage able to share practices and resources amongst them, the centres developed their own, divergent approaches to distributing their producers' videos guided by their specific circumstances. In the cases of both DMA and CMCM however, these approaches proved unstable, with both centres engaged in ongoing processes to maintain the distribution of these videos. For DMA, lack of sufficient resources for both their own internal efforts, and for the development of the non-profit OMP in general, meant that they were left with a solution that fell short of their requirements, and that was precarious because it depended on YouTube, whose interests, while aligned with DMA's by the end of the fieldwork, may not remain so because of the commercial logic that ultimately dictated its behaviour as an actor. For CMCM, lack of internal resource and the loss of a non-profit actor also impacted its online distribution assemblage, leading to it not functioning during the 2016/17 fieldwork while it awaited a new component for its cable television operations that would allow the remaining components to function together again.

The agency of the CACMX producers during both periods of fieldwork was typically significantly constrained. One factor contributing to this was the volume and complexity of the work required to construct and maintain their distribution assemblages, which was compounded by their inability to obtain adequate support, either because of the difficulties they had with volunteers or the lack of funds to pay for such support. This often meant that the implementation of adequate distribution solutions was delayed and inadequate solutions had to be tolerated for a time or indefinitely, that some platforms were not exploited to their full potential or just fell by the wayside, or that completed videos simply did not get uploaded. Other factors constraining the producers' agency were the policies and configurations of the platforms they used, which they had very little power to change. Overall, while their assemblages did afford them some agency with regard to distributing videos and the different outcomes they sought from doing this, it was significantly less than most had hoped for or tried to attain. This finding is unsurprising when considered within ANT and Assemblage Theory contexts: Being an actor in an assemblage does not mean being "in control" or "master" of a situation, since "an actor does not act alone", but rather in "relation to other actors" (Law and Mol 2008, 58), where the top-down effect of the assemblage constrain some capacities of its component actors while enabling others.

Notes

1 The Digital Arts Service Corps was an organization that placed volunteers within public media and technology organizations to "create and support specific capacity-building projects" (Digital Arts Service Corps 2017). Its funding ultimately derived from a US federal government agency, the Corporation for National and Community Service.

2 The community media centres were themselves complex assemblages, although this chapter is only concerned with their activities related to the online distribution of the public access television producers' videos, and so will not explore this aspect of them here: As we saw in Chapter 2, these centres could consist of up to three different television channels, a radio station, and various online spaces, which required a complex network of a wide range of people, machines, and other things to operate and maintain.

3 Deborah was not aware of the YouTube partner programme, which allowed users who were members of the programme to upload videos of any length.

4 This was a pane on the YouTube website where thumbnails of videos related to the one the user was currently viewing in the main pane of the website were displayed.

5 These components of course continued to exist as parts of other assemblages, but only as subsets, and nowhere all together. For example, the producers, their videos, and their third-party hosting platforms continued to exist within the producers' own distribution assemblages.

References

Callon, Michel. 1986. "Some Elements of a Sociology of Translation: The Domestication of the Scallops and St Brieuc Fishermen." In *Power, Action and Belief*, edited by J. Law, 196–232. London: Routledge and Kegan Paul.

DeLanda, Manuel. 2006a. "Deleuzian Social Ontology and Assemblage Theory." In *Deleuze and the Social*, edited by M. Fuglsang and B.M. Sørensen, 250–266. Edinburgh: Edinburgh University Press.

DeLanda, Manuel. 2006b. *A New Philosophy of Society: Assemblage Theory and Social Complexity*. London: Continuum (Kindle Edition).

DeLanda, Manuel. 2010. *Deleuze: History and Science*. New York: Atropos.

DeLanda, Manuel. 2011. *Philosophy and Simulation: The Emergence of Synthetic Reason*. London: Continuum (Kindle Edition).

Deleuze, Gilles, and Claire Parnet. 2006. *Dialogues II*. London: Continuum.

Digital Arts Service Corps. 2017. *Digital Arts Service Corps*, [cited October 9 2017]. Available from http://digitalartscorps.org/.

Environmental Voices. 2010. *About Us*, [cited July 7 2012]. Available from www.environmentalvoices.org/html/about.html.

Gane, Nicholas. 2004. *The Future of Social Theory*. London: Continuum.

Latour, Bruno. 1987. *Science in Action: How to Follow Scientists and Engineers through Society*. Cambridge, MA: Harvard University Press.

Latour, Bruno. 2005. *Reassembling the Social*. Oxford: Oxford University Press.

Law, John. 2003. Traduction/Trahison: Notes on ANT. www.lancaster.ac.uk/sociology/research/publications/papers/law-traduction-trahison.pdf.

Law, John, and Annemarie Mol. 2008. "The Actor-Enacted: Cumbrian Sheep in 2001." In *Material Agency: Towards a Non-anthropocentric Approach*, edited by Carl Knappett and Lambros Malafouris, 57–77. New York: Springer.

7 Conclusion
The Limits of Agency

The previous three chapters have provided detailed descriptions and analysis of how and why the different producer groups distributed their videos on the Internet, focusing on the dynamics surrounding the often complex and problematic assemblages of humans and machines they constructed for this purpose. These chapters showed that the groups' specific reasons and methods reflected their particular objectives and circumstances, which sometimes varied considerably not only between the groups but also between individuals within a group. They also, however, contained more generalizable findings, which were consistent with those of other studies that employed an assemblage-based theoretical framework to analyse digital media, and these included their observations concerning the distributed nature of agency (Salovaara 2015), the provisional nature of digital media assemblages (Rizzo 2015), and how human cultural practices in these contexts are socio-technical hybrids, where humans not only shape their tools, but are also shaped by them (Adamopoulos et al. 2014; Langlois 2013). A central question running through these chapters concerned the groups' and individual producers' agency, which was touched on in these chapters, and which will be explored at length here, with a focus on how the power relations that existed within their assemblages, and the work they had to perform in distributing their videos, limited their agency.

Buckingham (2009, 41–43) notes that "one of the recurring claims about amateur media production is the idea that it can permit a form of democratization of media. Successive generations of political and academic commentators have asserted that gaining access to the 'means of production' would empower individuals", further noting that such claims "have significantly resurfaced with the advent of the Internet". Buckingham then goes on to review some of Henry Jenkins's arguments in this vein, taking them as representative of this position, including his view that "digital technology has overcome many of the obstacles that led to the marginalisation of previous amateur film-making, partly because of the ... ease with which such material can be distributed online". In response to this position, Buckingham argues that "the crucial question here, however, is the extent to which ... this amounts to a form of 'empowerment' – and indeed, what that might mean", cautioning that "activity" should not be confused with "agency".

The findings from the previous three chapters provide some answers to Buckingham's question: Turning to the definitional aspect of the question first, "empowerment" in the context of the ethnography chapters was not addressed in the abstract or in general terms, but related instead to the specific objectives of each group, or in many cases to the objectives of the individual producers within these groups. For example, to understand whether the Internet empowered visionOntv, the answer requires an evaluation of the extent to which it allowed them to achieve their objectives as video makers, which in their case primarily concerned using the Internet to foster communities of social change. To understand whether it empowered Georgia however, the fan video maker who reluctantly adopted the Internet, requires an appeal to a different criterion, which was whether it allowed her to maintain the audience she previously reached using DVDs without her videos being readily accessible to others.

With this in mind, what we saw in the preceding chapters was that the Internet empowered the producers to achieve their objectives to varying degrees. For example, visionOntv were not able to achieve their primary objective and eventually decided to abandon it, although through their use of the Internet, they were able to achieve some of their intermediate and secondary goals, such as distributing large numbers of activist videos and training others to be activist video makers. The fans, on the other hand, generally had more modest objectives and typically saw Internet video distribution technologies as a way to integrate and simplify their community activities, or as a way of reaching a larger audience beyond their community, both of which they were largely successful in achieving. The CACMX producers fell somewhere in between the other two groups with respect to the degree the Internet empowered them, achieving their objectives to some degree, although the extent varied depending on their specific circumstances.

Understanding why some producers and groups were more successful than others at achieving their objectives related not only to the ambitiousness of their objectives, but also of course to their agency, or more precisely, in the theoretical context of this book, to the agency of the video distribution assemblages of which they were a part. The assessment of these different assemblages' agency in the preceding chapters required a detailed examination of the relationships that existed between their components and of how these relationships changed over time. This examination showed that these components constrained and enabled each other in different ways when they interacted, and also that the properties of the assemblages emerging as a result of these interactions sometimes acted to enable and constrain their components too. From this analysis, we saw that the producers, acting in concert with the other components, had the power to engage in certain activities that moved them towards their goals, but we also saw that these activities were often constrained by these other components, or by the top-down effects of the assemblages' emergent properties.

While the nature of these constraints largely varied depending upon the specific circumstances of the groups or individual producers, many of them resulted from the fact that the Internet platforms they used were actors and assemblages in their own right and therefore, rather than being dutiful components of their assemblages, were sometimes a source of conflict and instability. In situations such as these, rather than behaving as "intermediaries" (Latour 2005, 39) that simply transported videos, texts, and the other artefacts of the producers' and their audiences' activities to other nodes in an assemblage without change or interruption, and thereby fading into the background, their specificity as assemblages came to the fore and had to be engaged with. For example, the platforms sometimes actively prevented the producers' attempts to use them in a particular way, such as when videos were taken down, blocked, or muted or when accounts were closed or suspended, which was experienced by many of the producers in the previous chapters on different platforms. The dynamic and precarious nature of these platforms was also a source of instability for the groups' assemblages. This sometimes manifested when the platforms changed how they operated, resulting in them no longer interacting with other components as desired, such as how changes to Facebook's post filtering algorithms meant that visionOntv's posts were reaching fewer of its Facebook friends than previously, thereby reducing its audience, or when changes to Blip meant that videos embedded from it into Live-Journal no longer played. It also manifested when the platforms ceased to function at all, either temporarily, such as when LiveJournal came under denial-of-service attacks, or when they permanently closed down as was experienced, for example, with iMeem, Blip, and Miro Community, amongst others.

Although the groups had little power to change the constraining properties of the third-party proprietary platforms they used, even the open-source platforms often proved insufficiently malleable for their needs, since the work required to transform them in the desired way was either technically or quantitatively beyond their capabilities. This meant that the groups were either unable to develop all the functionality they required, such as with Archive of Our Own's lack of video hosting functionality, or unable to develop the functionality to a level that was sufficient to interest users in adopting the platform, such as with visionOntv's use of Liferay's Community Edition and the issues related to its social networking functionality. This lack of capacity and technical skills also meant that even when the groups' tried to developed their own platforms from the ground up, these were either unsuccessful, as with the public access producer Frank's attempts in 2011/12 to develop his own website, or had limited functionality, as with the websites of the vidding community, which did not allow video streaming.

The consequences of all these constraining factors meant that the groups' assemblages included a combination of platforms that were chosen to compensate for each other's limitations, and for their capacity to "co-function" (Deleuze and Parnet 2006, 52) with each other and the assemblages' other components in such a way as to enable the groups' producers to achieve their goals as video makers. In spite of this, the agency of the groups' assemblages typically fell short of their requirements, as they were often unable to overcome the constraints caused by the different platforms' limited functionality, or to adequately address the instability introduced by those platforms. Part of this resulted from the groups' increasing reliance on proprietary third-party platforms, which they had little power to transform or prevent from unilaterally removing themselves either partly or completely from their assemblages, but which they needed to supplement or replace their own development endeavours. Particular concern in this regard focused on the groups' reliance on a dwindling number of large commercial platforms, which had come about because of the failure or inadequacies of the smaller commercial and non-commercial platforms they had previously used, and their reluctance to use those that survived because of concerns about their long-term viability. This was in spite of the antipathy expressed towards these large commercial platforms and the considerable effort that went into exploring and developing alternatives. This finding furthers our understanding of the kinds of processes that have led to these platforms coming to dominate the Internet and provides an additional perspective to critiques that reach similar conclusions using different approaches (for example Fuchs (2015, 229), which was discussed in Chapter 2).

The volume and technical complexity of the work required to build and maintain the groups' distribution assemblages also acted to limit their agency. This was touched on above in relation to the work required to transform the open-source platforms they used, but as we saw in the preceding chapters, the processes required to enrol and stabilize their assemblages' other human and technological components also required significant and ongoing work. Sometimes the volume or specialist nature of this work meant that it could not be carried out, or at least not to the required degree, or that carrying it out was sufficiently burdensome that it delayed the groups from achieving their overall goals. Examples of some of these situations included Antonio's ability to promote his public access television videos online being limited by his lack of digital marketing skills, and visionOntv's difficulties in making the RSS feeds they used in their assemblage function as desired. The burden of this work was amplified by the fact that the producers' video making and distribution activities were typically a sideline or hobby for them, and many preferred to devote what time they had available to making rather than distributing videos. In such circumstances, even the general maintenance work carried out by all the groups as they went about stabilizing their assemblages, which included uploading videos, making posts, replying to comments, responding to takedown notices, fixing broken connections between different platforms, replacing malfunctioning platforms, and re-uploading videos amongst other things, also represented a not insignificant call on the groups' time, and some producers in fact did not have time to perform all the required maintenance tasks, which limited the functionality of their assemblages or left them in a precarious state.

While critical academic debate concerning digital labour focuses on its exploitative nature (Freedman 2012, 87–88; Fuchs 2015, 229), the above analysis draws our attention to how its demands can act to limit the agency of non-professional video makers in some circumstances. This observation, combined with the earlier one concerning how the groups' activities concerning the development of open-source and their own platforms were constrained by their lack of capacity and technical skills, show that while the Internet may provide non-professional video makers with varying degrees of agency to achieve their goals, they operate at considerable disadvantages when compared to their professional counterparts, who are often able to draw upon organizational resources to assist them in the distribution process.

The above discussion of agency focused on the online aspects of the groups' distribution activities, in response to Buckingham's question concerning the empowering nature of the Internet, but as we saw in the preceding chapters, these activities also had offline aspects. During the 2011/12 period of the fieldwork, at least some members in each group included offline components in their assemblages that they considered an important part of their distribution practices, or had aspirations towards doing so. These included showing videos at conventions, at training workshops, at activist screenings, and on cable television. By 2016/17 however, various changes to the groups' circumstances had meant that these offline distribution methods had declined in importance for some groups, or at least for some of their members, although it was difficult to discern at that particular juncture whether this restricted the agency of any of the producers. For example, although VividCon had announced that 2018 would be its last year of operation, with the spatially deterritorializing effects of the Internet on fan video viewing practices given as a primary reason for its closure, vidUKon continued to thrive, and planning was underway for the 2019 launch of a new convention, FanWorks, which would feature fan videos as well as other kinds of fan works.

Within the context of the theoretical framework of this study, assessments of agency are primarily grounded in the specific circumstances of the video makers since it derives from the properties that emerge from the enabling and constraining effects of the interacting components within the particular assemblages they built in pursuit of their goals.

Following Latour (1988, 157–158, 174), explanations concerning their agency are therefore "tailor-made" to those circumstances, rather than being imposed ready-made and top-down by a theory, although such bottom-up explanations come at the expense of being unable to provide the more generalized type of explanations that are possible with the other approach. Therefore, while we did see in the preceding chapters that the groups typically had insufficient resources and power to build and maintain the assemblages they desired to achieve their goals, and that this limited their agency, the degree to which this occurred, its impact on their activities, and indeed the amount of concern this caused them varied greatly from group to group, and from producer to producer.

References

Adamopoulos, Arthur, Martin Dick, and Bill Davey. 2014. "Web Tools as Actors: The Case of Online Investing." In *Technological Advancements and the Impact of Actor-Network Theory*, edited by Tatnall Arthur, 252–259. Hershey, PA: IGI Global.

Buckingham, David. 2009. "A Commonplace Art? Amateur Media Production." In *Video Cultures: Media Technology and Everyday Creativity*, edited by David Buckingham and Rebekah Willett, 23–50. New York: Palgrave Macmillan.

Deleuze, Gilles, and Claire Parnet. 2006. *Dialogues II*. London: Continuum.

Freedman, D. 2012. " Web 2.0 and the Death of the Blockbuster Economy." In *Misunderstanding the Internet*, edited by J. Curran, N. Fenton, and D. Freedman. Abingdon: Routledge.

Fuchs, Christian. 2015. *Culture and Economy in the Age of Social Media*. New York: Routledge.

Langlois, Ganaele. 2013. "Participatory Culture and the New Governance of Communication: The Paradox of Participatory Media." *Television & New Media* no. 14 (2):91–105.

Latour, Bruno. 1988. "The Politics of Explanation: An Alternative." In *Knowledge and Reflexivity, New Frontiers in the Sociology of Knowledge*, edited by Steve Woolgar, 155–176. London: Sage.

Latour, Bruno. 2005. *Reassembling the Social*. Oxford: Oxford University Press.

Rizzo, Teresa. 2015. "FCJ-177 Television Assemblages." *The Fibreculture Journal* (24):106–126.

Salovaara, Inka. 2015. "Media Spaces of Fluid Politics Participatory Assemblages and Networked Narratives." *Media Transformations* no. 11:10–29.

Index

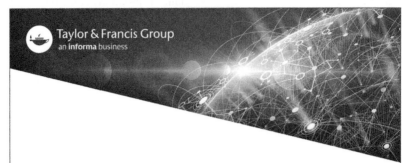

For Product Safety Concerns and Information please contact our EU
representative GPSR@taylorandfrancis.com Taylor & Francis Verlag GmbH,
Kaufingerstraße 24, 80331 München, Germany

Printed and bound by CPI Group (UK) Ltd, Croydon, CR0 4YY
01/05/2025
01858513-0002